Edward T Hall

The Spanish Main

or Thirty days on the Caribbean

Edward T Hall

The Spanish Main
or Thirty days on the Caribbean

ISBN/EAN: 9783743321755

Manufactured in Europe, USA, Canada, Australia, Japa

Cover: Foto ©ninafisch / pixelio.de

Manufactured and distributed by brebook publishing software (www.brebook.com)

Edward T Hall

The Spanish Main

THE

SPANISH MAIN;

OR,

THIRTY DAYS ON THE CARIBBEAN.

BY EDWARD T. HALL.

ILLUSTRATIONS FROM THE AUTHOR'S PHOTOGRAPHS, ENGRAVED BY MISS JULIA M. HALL.

THE SPANISH MAIN.

CHAPTER I.

A Voyage to the Spanish Main.

I WAS born in the City of New York, and spent nearly the whole of the early part of my life in that great metropolis.

In my school-boy days it was my infinite delight to roam and linger along the docks and watch the stately ships as they came and went, or as they lay at their piers discharging or taking in cargo. As I gazed at the tapering masts and spars and saw the sailors running up and down the shrouds and ratlins like squirrels, or clinging to the cross-yards like spiders on a wall, I wished that I could be a sailor. But as I grew older, and by education came to know the hardships and privations of a sailor's life as well as its perils, and more especially as I reflected upon his necessitated seclusion from the society of those he dearly loves, and which tends so much toward making up the sum of human happiness, I was easily persuaded to relinquish the desire to adopt a seafaring life.

But my love for the ocean and my longings to visit foreign shores grew no less as the years sped on. I fed my passion on the entrancing sea novels of Cooper and Maryatt. Like as Claude Melnotte said to his Pauline, "We'll read no books that are not tales of love, that we may smile to think how poorly eloquence of words translates the poetry of hearts like ours," so did I seek to read only such books as were tales of the sea, and dream of that happy time—that I felt sure would come to me—when I could gratify the yearnings of my heart.

But, as if to mock at my youthful hopes, Dame Fortune decreed that I should live for many years an inland life, deprived even of a glimpse of the ocean, or a sight of those gallant ships which bring from afar for us the products of other lands, and scatter the wealth of all climes broadcast among the sons of men.

Thus it was that middle-life had come and gone before I was able in any degree to indulge the passion which had so early animated my breast, and which has never ceased to burn brightly on the altar of my fondest hopes.

But there finally came a time when I could lay aside temporarily every year the cares of business, and enjoy with keenest zest the ever-changing experience of ocean voyages and visits to strange countries.

It is my purpose at the present time to give some account of a voyage to the Spanish Main, which I had the pleasure of making in the early spring months of 1887.

At one o'clock on Wednesday, March 2d, I was a passenger on the iron steamship "Philadelphia," of the Red "D" Line, which sailed from Pier 36, East River, in the port of New York. The day was an exceptionally fine one for this season of the year. The sun shone brightly and the air was as balmy as in the leafy month of June. A tug-boat helped us to swing around toward the bay against a strong flood tide, and in a few minutes we were steaming majestically along under the great bridge that spans the East River and unites the City of New York to her sister City of Brooklyn. Soon we were rapidly passing the now famous statue of "Liberty Enlightening the World," sometimes familiarly called "Mademoiselle Bartholdi." When we reached Sandy Hook our good-looking young pilot, after courteously shaking hands with the captain and first officer, swung himself lightly over the rail, and by a rope-ladder descended to a small row-boat which had put off from a pilot-boat, on a signal from our mast-head, to take him from our steamer.

To a landsman the transit from a great ocean steamer to a little row-boat, which bobs up and down on the waves like an egg-shell, would be an awkward feat to accomplish, and might easily result in a broken limb or a sea-water bath, but to our pilot, with his experience and coolness and strength of arm, it appears to be as easy as "rolling off from a log." He descends the rope-ladder to within a few feet of the heaving waters, but is in no hurry to let go. He bides his time until a wave brings the little boat up to the proper position for his purpose, when he drops lightly down and in a twinkling is in the stern-sheets, with his hand on the tiller. His cheery voice shouts, "Give way, my lads!" and the oarsmen row him quickly away from the great steamer.

Now the captain takes charge, and our course is laid south, one and a quarter points east, which course we will continue to hold for several days and nights till we approach the islands of St. Domingo and Porto Rico, between which we are to sail, taking care to avoid two smaller islands lying between these two greater ones just named, and which are called, respectively, "Mona Island" and "Monita Island;" that is to say, "Monkey Island" and "Little Monkey Island."

This course between these islands is designated on the charts as the "Mona Passage," and here our course will be changed to a more southerly one, and we will enter the Caribbean Sea. Thence we will shape our course a little west of south for the tropical island of Curacao. This island is one of that great group that come under the general name of the West Indies, but it is more particularly known as one of the

Caribbee Islands. It also belongs to that group known as the "Leeward" Islands, in contradistinction to a group farther eastward, known as the "Windward" Islands. So it is proper to speak of Curacao as one of the West India Islands, or as one of the Carib or Caribbee Islands, or as one of the Leeward Islands, either expression being correct.

And now, while we are bowling along at the rate of twelve or thirteen knots an hour, I will bring this first chapter to a close, and in my state-room bed shut my eyes and woo the drowsy god of sleep, while listening to the waves swashing against our steamer as she proudly plows her way through them. The majesty of the ocean ceases not when the eye is closed upon its heaving bosom. The rushing sound of its many waters, when the head is on the pillow, makes its impress on the reflective mind as deeply as to gaze on its restless billows.

Here is a beautiful ode to the Sea, written by a German poet:

To The Sea.

Thou boundless, shining, glorious Sea.
With ecstasy I gaze on thee;
Joy, joy to him whose early beam
Kisses thy lip, bright Ocean-stream!

Thanks for the thousand hours, old Sea,
Of sweet communion held with thee:
Oft as I gazed, thy billowy roll
Woke the deep feelings of my soul.

Drunk with the joy, thou deep-toned Sea,
My spirit swells to heaven with thee;
Or, sinking with thee, seeks the gloom
Of nature's deep, mysterious tomb.

At evening, when the sun grows red,
Descending to his watery bed,
The music of the murmuring deep
Soothes e'en the weary earth to sleep.

Then listens thee the evening star,
So sweetly glancing from afar;
And Luna hears thee when she breaks
Her light in million-colored flakes.

Oft when the noonday heat is o'er,
I seek with joy the breezy shore,
Sink on thy boundless, billowy breast,
And cheer me with refreshing rest.

The poet, child of heavenly birth,
Is suckled by the mother earth;
But thy blue bosom, holy Sea,
Cradles his infant fantasy.

The old blind minstrel on the shore
Stood listening thy eternal roar,
And golden ages, long gone by,
Swept bright before his spirit's eye.

On wing of swan the holy flame
Of melodies celestial came,
And Iliad and Odyssey
Rose to the music of the Sea.

—Frederick Leopold, Count of Stolberg.

CHAPTER II.

AT SEA—OUR STEAMER AND HER OFFICERS.

AS I commence this chapter I do not forget that a great many people who, in these days of comfortable traveling facilities, and of "Cook's Tours" and "Raymond's Excursions" to all parts of the world, are familiar with the average ocean steamer and its characteristics. To these, my account of the steamer "Philadelphia," and her officers, will doubtless possess but little interest. But I also reflect that there is a far greater proportion who are unfamiliar with the details of the construction of these great steamships that transport with comfort and safety so many hundreds of thousands of the members of the human family to all parts of the world, over that great, free and universal highway, the ocean.

To this class of my readers I will give a few items of the dimensions and construction of the steamer "Philadelphia," of the Red "D" Line, plying between the City of New York and Puerto Cabello and La Guayra in Venezuela, also stopping at the island of Curacao. I shall also venture to say something of her officers.

The "Philadelphia" was built by William Cramp & Sons, of Philadelphia. Her length over all is 283 feet 6 inches; length on water line, 270 feet 9 inches; beam, 35 feet; depth of hold to main deck, 20 feet 6 inches; depth of hold to upper deck, 28 feet 3 inches; tonnage, 2,100 gross. She is constructed of iron. Forward are the anchors and chains, anchor crane with attachments and capstan, which is worked from steam windlass below.

There are three hatches for cargo, each provided with iron hatch cover, gummed and secured with strong iron dogs, making them absolutely water-tight. The pilot-house on the upper deck is provided with steam steering-gear of the most approved style, which can be disconnected should it be desired, and the vessel then steered by hand. In addition, she is also provided with a wheel aft.

The captain's cabin, aft of the pilot-house, is finished in hard wood, and possesses every convenience for comfort. First and second officers' rooms adjoin. Following these are two state-rooms on each side, abaft of which is a stairway leading to the main deck. Aft of the after-hatch is a deck-house, containing the social hall, with main entrance to saloon, then six state-rooms, three on each side, and after these a large and comfortable smoking-room. She is provided with six life-boats, swung on iron frames overhead, so as to allow an unobstructed promenade on the upper deck, and two life-rafts placed on the roof of the deck-house. Seats are fitted along the rail on each side from the pilot-house aft.

The saloon on the main deck extends the entire width of the vessel, thus insuring good light and ventilation. The dining tables, seven in number, are arranged three on each side, and one in the center, those on the side being placed athwartship, thus enabling each passenger to occupy or vacate his seat without disturbing others. Handsome sideboards are placed on each side. Adjoining the dining-saloon there are nineteen state-rooms, which, with the tier on the upper deck, accommodate sixty-four first-class passengers. In the rear are ladies' and gentlemen's toilet-rooms and two bath-rooms. The social hall, saloon and state-rooms are hard-wood finish, pannelling of mahogany, oak and ash, the upholstery being of plush.

The pantry and kitchen are fitted with steam tables and all the appliances of a first-class hotel. The officers' quarters, for the engineers, stewards and purser, are on the main deck, with the mail-room adjoining the latter. The officers' mess-room is finished in hard wood. Ample accommodations are provided for second-class passengers and crew, also for ice-houses and store-rooms. The hold is divided by five water-tight bulkheads. Each compartment is ventilated by air shafts leading to the interior of the smoke-stack, by means of which a powerful draught is created, thereby preventing condensation from warm air in coming from the tropics.

The machinery consists of a vertical compound surface condensing engine, with cylinders 32 and 61 inches diameter respectively, stroke 3 feet. The engine is fitted with all modern improvements, such as steam reversing gear, governor, feed water heater, filter, etc. Two duplex donkey pumps are conveniently located, with connections to bilge, sea condenser, boilers, tanks and all parts of the vessel for fire-hose. The boilers, two in number, are made of extra quality tested steel, 14 feet in diameter, 12½ feet long; each has three furnaces. The working pressure of steam is ninety pounds, though they were tested to one hundred and eighty pounds. In construction, outfit and finish this ship is a first-class specimen of American marine architecture, and rates 100 A1 XX for twenty years in British Lloyd's.

Her officers are as follows:

Commander,	Capt. SAMUEL HESS.
First Officer,	WILLIAM A. WILKINSON.
Second Officer,	JOHN SKELLING.
Chief Engineer,	GEORGE W. CAMPBELL.
Purser,	WILLIAM HOWE.
Steward,	JOHN HARDY.

Besides these there are two assistant engineers, three oilers, seven firemen, three coal passers, two quartermasters, one boatswain, one carpenter, six able seamen, five colored deckhands, six colored table-waiters, three cooks, one pantry-man, one messman, one porter, and last, though not least, one stewardess, "fair, fat and forty," who is the ministering angel to the lady passengers, either when they are really seasick, or merely "afraid they are going to be." The stereotyped smile which perpetually illumines her "seven-by-nine" countenance, carries assurance and sweet hope to all tremulous souls who dread the tribute that old Neptune sometimes demands from over-loaded stomachs. I cannot think of omitting, at this opportune place, that old familiar tribute to woman:

> "Oh, woman, in our hours of ease,
> Uncertain, coy and hard to please,
> When pain and anguish wring the brow;
> A ministering angel thou!"

Capt. Samuel Hess is a most excellent type of a true American sailor. Born in Philadelphia and coming from good old Quaker stock, he had the benefit of an early religious training and a good education. But he was bound to be a sailor, and actually went to sea as a cabin-boy before he was twelve years old! He has followed the sea ever since—a period of forty years. He rapidly rose in the profession and has been the captain of many vessels and sailed to nearly every part of the globe. Bluff and hearty in manner, rigid in discipline, though kind-hearted and just, he is always a gentleman and endears himself to all classes, whether they are directly under his authority or are his passengers. Being the senior captain in this line, he is the commodore of the fleet, and has command of its newest and finest vessel.

Captain Hess is a strictly temperate man and requires that his officers shall, while on duty, be the same. It is such men as Captain Hess that we pin our faith to when we embark on a voyage which *may* be fraught with danger, requiring the best seamanship, long experience, cool judgment and unclouded brain, undaunted courage, unflagging watchfulness and great physical endurance.

When I doff my clothes, and, donning my *robe de nuit*, lie down to pleasant slumbers in my little bed, I feel that I am safe, not only in the general Providential care that is over us all during the silent watches of the night, but also in that special providence which I feel is guarding me in the person of our most excellent and watchful commander.

I have said that Captain Hess has followed the sea for forty years, but this is not strictly correct, for there was an interval of eight months during the year 1865 that he followed something else more treacherous even than the ocean. How I came to know it is as follows: When I was first introduced to him he asked me where I was from. I told him from Pennsylvania.

"What part of Pennsylvania?"

"From that part called the Oil Regions."

"From the Oil Regions, eh!"

A feeble smile played around the corners of the captain's mouth as he made this last remark, and I immediately knew that he was one of that innumerable army who, in the early days of the history of Petroleum, had "been there," and had put much more money in the ground than they had ever taken out. Oh, I meet them all over, in Mexico, on the Pacific Slope, in Cuba, in Florida, on the coast of Maine, in the Lake Superior region, and on the bosom of the broad Atlantic.

The captain's experience was no exception to the general rule. He came, he saw, but he didn't conquer! *Au contraire*, he dropped a few thousands in a few months and then returned complacently to his vocation, "sailing the ocean blue," just as if nothing had happened!

He laughs over the episode, just as I find all sensible men do after a lapse of twenty years, when Time, the great healer, has assuaged the grief, and Dame Fortune has, in other and more certain channels, compensated for the losses that inexperience and mistaken zeal in their calculation of an "unknown quantity" brought upon them.

Captain Hess' first officer, Mr. Wilkinson, is also a life-long sailor. He was born in Pennsylvania, in the town of Bristol, and has had a wide and eventful experience on the ocean. He cannot be called a handsome man, and yet he is not homely enough to stop a clock! What he lacks in beauty he more than makes up in pleasing manners, and is a general favorite with all the passengers. To him I am indebted for much information, which I hope will be interesting to my readers.

In thinking of the invariable politeness of all the officers of this ship, I cannot help saying to myself, "Like master, like man," for when I went to the office of the owners of this line, Messrs. Boulton, Bliss & Dallett, No. 71 Wall street, to procure my state-room, I was treated with the utmost courtesy and kindness. All inquiries were cordially answered and many things suggested that would tend to make the voyage more thoroughly enjoyable and satisfactory.

How different is this from the crusty manners assumed by many officials clothed in a little brief authority! How often have I been made to feel like a detected pickpocket when making a polite inquiry of some of these offensive clerks and agents! Oh, when they come to receive their final reward for all the deeds done in the body, may it be their doom to be perpetually snubbed by all the dirty little imps of Hades!

This is our second day out of New York. The skies continue clear and cloudless, and the air is so soft and balmy that we are sitting about the decks without overcoats and feeling thoroughly comfortable. In the evening the moon, "pale empress of the night," rides high in the heavens, and the sweet glimmer of the stars upon the water's wide expanse, make a scene of loveliness, as well as grandeur, and I sit in my steamer chair gazing and dreaming long after the other passengers have gone to rest. I recall the words of Lorenzo and Jessica at Belmont:

> The moon shines bright: In such a night as this,
> When the sweet wind did gently kiss the trees,
> And they did make no noise; in such a night,
> Troilus, methinks, mounted the Trojan walls,
> And sigh'd his soul toward the Grecian tents,
> Where Cressid lay that night.
>
>   In such a night,
> Did Thisbe fearfully o'ertrip the dew,
> And saw the lion's shadow ere himself,
> And ran dismay'd away.
>
>   In such a night,
> Stood Dido, with a willow in her hand,
> Upon the wild sea-banks, and waved her love
> To come again to Carthage.
>
>   In such a night,
> Medea gather'd the enchanted herbs,
> That did renew old Æson.
>
>   In such a night,
> Did Jessica steal from the wealthy Jew,
> And with an unthrift love did run from Venice,
> As far as Belmont.
>
>   And in such a night,
> Did young Lorenzo swear he loved her well,
> Stealing her soul with many vows of faith,
> And ne'er a true one.
>
>   And in such a night,
> Did pretty Jessica, like a little shrew,
> Slander her love, and he forgave it her.
>
>   —*Shakespeare.*

CHAPTER III.

Lost at Sea—And Some of My Fellow-Travelers.

"YES," said Mr. Wilkinson, one night as I paced the deck with him during his watch, "you may well say that a sailor's life is one of hardship and peril. I read in the Good Book that when David was beset on all sides by the soldiers of King Saul who sought to take his life, he said to Jonathan, 'Surely, there is but a step between me and death,' and I think how true this is of every sailor's life! A single misstep may at any time plunge him into the relentless ocean, or fling him from the giddy mast to an almost certain death on the deck below. Yes, as you say, our life is often held by a single thread, and, as an illustration of this, I must tell you of a tragic incident that I witnessed once on shipboard.

"It was about twelve years ago," continued the chief officer, "when I was on the steamship 'Pennsylvania,' of the American Line, plying between Philadelphia and Liverpool. Old Captain Thomas Harris was her commander, a bluff old sea-dog, but as big-hearted a man as I ever knew. When he died a few years ago that line lost its best captain. But, as I was saying, it was on the 'Pennsylvania' on an outward voyage in June, the third day out, in the neighborhood of the 'Banks,' we were running along with a fine breeze from the westward, with all sails set, and making twelve to thirteen knots an hour. It was my watch on deck, but I had gone below to work up my reckoning, when suddenly the engine gong struck the signal to stop the ship. I ran up the companion-way bareheaded as the cry of 'Man overboard!' rang in my ears. I shouted, 'Clear away the starboard forward boat,' and it took but a moment or two to do so, and, as it was being lowered, I and the crew of six leaped in. By this time the engine was backing, although the steamer was still forging ahead quite rapidly.

"As the boat struck the water we unhooked the falls, and Captain Harris, who was on the bridge, shouted to me, 'There he is, Wilkinson,' pointing in the direction of where the poor fellow was fighting against his fate. As I stood up in the stern of the boat with my hand on the tiller, I could see, as the boat rose on the huge waves, the poor man away off to the leeward, struggling in the waves, and a number of sea-birds circling about him. My men, you may be sure, pulled with a will, and soon we came to the spot to find only the man's hat, he having sunk beneath the waves and was seen no more!

"We rowed all about for a half an hour or more and then returned sorrowfully to the ship. Not till we were again on board did I know who the poor victim was, but then I learned that it was Henry Hargrave, one of our able seamen, who had shipped with us for the first time a few days before at Philadelphia, having but just returned from a voyage to the East Indies. The way the accident happened, was like this: He was standing on the rail of the deck, reaching up and lacing the canvas cover on one of the life-boats, which was in the davits and chocks just above his head. In pulling one of the laces it broke, and the poor fellow, losing his balance, fell backward into the sea.

"Of course the occurrence cast a gloom over the ship for a day or two, but on a large steamer with a crew of an hundred men, and with several hundred passengers, such things are soon forgotten. So, you see, this sailor's life actually hung on a single thread, and the thread broke!

" But now I must tell you what to me was the hardest part of the whole affair. When we got back to Philadelphia, and the ship was made fast to the dock, I hurried on shore to see my family. At the big gate going off from the dock I was accosted by a young girl of twelve or thirteen years of age, who was accompanied by an old and feeble-looking man. She said to me, in a very pleasant voice, ' Do you belong on the steamer ' Pennsylvania' ? '

" I said, ' Yes, Miss, what do you want ? '

" She replied, ' My brother is a sailor on that ship, and just before he sailed on her he wrote to us that when he came back he would come home. We have not seen him for nine years. We live in Cincinnati, and we have come up here to meet him and take him home with us.'

" I said, ' What is your brother's name ? '

" She replied, ' Henry Hargrave.'

" The cold chills ran up and down my back, and I knew not what to say. I finally stammered out that there was no one by that name that came back with us, but that I would go on board and make inquiries and come and tell them. As I reached the ship I met Captain Harris going ashore, and related to him what had just taken place.

" He said to me, ' I can't bear to tell them, Mr. Wilkinson, and you will have to attend to it for me. Tell them that we left him very sick in the hospital at Liverpool, and then we can write and tell them the *truth* afterward.'

" So I had to go back and deceive them (but, as I thought, mercifully) in this way. I found that the mother had also come up from Cincinnati to meet her sailor-boy, and was then at the lodging-house awaiting his footstep. I took them to a more respectable lodging-house than they had been taken to by a runner, and advised them to start for home as soon as possible, promising to write to them as soon as I could about their son. I saw them safely on the cars the next day, and they went back home, sorrowfully, but still with hope that their dear boy would yet come home to them. In a day or two I wrote them a long letter, telling them the whole truth, and the purser sent to them the poor fellow's kit and what money he had in his chest—not much was it, I assure you, for poor Jack has too many temptations, and is too free with his money to ever save up much. Well, I have spun you a long yarn, and now, as it is eight bells, I will turn in for four hours."

The state-room next to mine, on the upper deck, was occupied by Mr. David Logan, a Scotchman of the most pronounced type. He has been a great traveler and there are probably but few men that have had as many peculiar and interesting experiences as he. I have sat for hours and listened to his adventures in many lands, while pursuing his vocation as a naturalist. He is forty-six years of age, was born in Paisley, Scotland, and came to America in 1852. In the year 1861 he started for the West Indies, and, after visiting many of these islands, and making large collections of insects, butterflies and orchids, he went to Central America and Honduras, and then to Old Mexico. He was gone on this trip nine years. He then went to Africa, and among the collections he made there, was a giant or Goliath beetle, a rare specimen, for which he received twenty pounds, or, in our money, one hundred dollars. His sales of specimens are generally made to the museums of England, they paying far better prices than museums or collectors in this country.

After his trip to Africa, he again went to Central America, and while there visited the remarkable and prehistoric ruins in Yucatan; his descriptions of which are exceedingly interesting. Mr. Logan is now on his way to Venezuela, which country he will certainly exhaust of beetles and all other insects, butterflies, and orchids—or, at least, two or three good specimens of each variety. Mr. Logan says that he has a standing offer of three thousand dollars for one particular variety of orchid, and he has great hopes that it is to be found in Venezuela.

Another of my fellow-voyagers was Mr. Angell of New York, a young man engaged in mercantile business although a graduate of Yale College. He, like myself, is traveling for pleasure, and will make the round trip on this steamer. He is an amateur entomologist, and so is Mr. Henry F. Rudloff, a German resident of Venezuela, who is a civil engineer, and is now returning on this steamer from a business visit to New York. A naturalist and two entomologists meeting on a steamer by mere chance, among a passenger list of only twenty, is quite a coincidence. It was a picnic to hear them talk bugs!

Among our passengers was a Spanish student returning from some college in the United States, to his home in the city of Caracas, the capital of Venezuela. Also another Spanish gentleman who, with his wife and sister-in-law, was returning to Venezuela from an extended tour through our country.

Then there were Mr. H. T. Livingston, an old retired merchant of New York City, a courtly gentleman, and his son, a young man of about thirty years of age, who were seeking a change of climate for the benefit of their health. Another pleasant traveler was a Mr. Davis, an American, who has large mining interests in Venezuela. We had but five lady passengers, and one of these was Miss N. who, with her father, was going to Curacao to try the air of that island for some lung trouble. Miss N. is a good musician, and after recovering from the effects of a slight attack of seasickness, she contributed largely to the enjoyment of our outward passage, by singing many of the dear old songs of our native land, and on the Sabbath leading us with voice and piano in the familiar hymns in which all citizens of a Christian land have a common interest, and in the singing of which I have always found brings together almost immediately, and in a most friendly manner, all American travelers.

There was but one other passenger whom I will mention particularly. About a half an hour before our steamer left her dock, as I stood watching the passengers as they came on board, a carriage drove up and a young man was helped out by the driver. A lady was in the carriage and the young man kissed her good-by through the door, as she did not alight. He wore a long English ulster which came down nearly to his feet, and his neck and face were closely muffled up with a shawl, although the day was warm. His trunk and satchel were taken by the porter to a state-room on deck, the second one from mine, and he slowly followed. He had his dinner brought to his state-room and I saw no more of him until the next morning. I then saluted him and asked how he had passed the night. He replied in a whisper that he had not slept so well in two months and then explained, very briefly, that he had lost his voice and he was going to the equator, if necessary, to try and find it. I expressed my sympathy, which was the more sincere as I had myself met with the same misfortune about twenty-five years ago. I told him not to try to talk, but that I would talk to him and would not expect any reply that would require him to use his vocal powers. I then related to him my experience and predicted that in his case, as it had occurred in mine, the voice would come back when he had been in a very hot climate a few days.

His name, as I learned from the purser, was Morrison, but who he was, or what his business, no one had any idea. A more silent man I never met and he seemed to shun every one except myself. He endured me, at any rate, with patience, and I continued to hold a very one-sided conversation with him at intervals for several days. On Sunday he came for the first time into the Social Hall and listened attentively to the hymns we sung, led by Miss X.

On Monday morning he returned my greeting with a decided smile, and I told him that he was looking much better, and that I expected to hear his voice by the time we reached Curacao. This is pronounced "Cure-a-so," with the accent on the last syllable, and he said he hoped it would also "cure a cold."

This feeble attempt at wit encouraged me to ask him if he could not help me by and by to bring out a little more talent in our passenger list. He made no response, but having "put my foot in it," I proceeded to ask him if he had any knowledge of music, and he replied "a little." I suggested, inquiringly, that perhaps he played on some instrument and he said he used to play the banjo slightly. I soon took occasion to inquire of the steward if any of the colored waiters had a banjo, and he said that one of them had. I hunted it up and had it made ready for use that evening.

After dinner at 6 P. M., the captain, who, by conversation, we had ascertained was what he styled a "salt-water astronomer," consented to give us a little talk about the stars. It was a most lovely night, and we all sat in a circle on the deck while Captain Hess, in a most interesting manner, pointed out to us the stars and constellations, and the Southern Cross and the "false cross," and in a very unassuming manner displayed a knowledge of the heavenly bodies that astonished us. Mr. Morrison, at my urgent solicitation, had joined us, and at the conclusion of the lecture I quietly placed the banjo across his knees and rather anxiously awaited the result. He looked up at me reproachfully but took up the instrument and tried its tone. In a moment he had it tuned and then he played it in a masterly manner. His auditors were so delighted that he was kept playing for nearly an hour, and it was unanimously voted that a new era of enjoyment had begun.

I shall have occasion to refer again to Mr. Morrison, and will only add at this time that he soon got over the blues, and when his voice did come to him a few days after this, he used it to our great amusement in singing some of the most rollicking and enjoyable songs that I ever listened to.

On Saturday morning, March 5th, the weather still being perfectly beautiful, we saw for the first time since leaving Sandy Hook, a vessel on our starboard bow. Here we are nearly nine hundred miles from New York, and until now have not seen a single vessel! Does not this give one a realizing sense of the immensity of the ocean? To be sure our course is rather out from the usual course of steamers and sailing vessels to the southern ports. But here away off to the westward we now plainly see a full-rigged ship. She shows up beautifully through the spy-glass, and one of our passengers pronounces her to be a United States man-of-war—one of the school or training-ships, that are cruising in these waters. Soon two other sails are descried right ahead of us and two more on the port bow, making five in all for us to look at through the spy-glasses and field-glasses.

About this time the captain succeeds, with a line and large hooks, in pulling on board a fragment of a sea-plant or weed on which the little white coral insect is plainly seen with the naked eye.

Now the great full-rigged ship passes down the horizon almost out of sight, and the captain says she is but a merchant ship and not a man-of-war. Then sail along within a mile of us a three-masted schooner and two barks, all bound, we presume, for North America, under a fine northeast breeze. On one of the barks I counted twenty sails all set and full of wind. Where these beautiful white-winged ships are from, or whither bound, are matters of pure conjecture. I am reminded of T. Buchanan Read's beautiful poem called "Drifting," a verse or two of which read thus:

> Yon deep bark goes
> Where traffic blows,
> From lands of sun to lands of snows;—
> This happier one,
> Its course is run
> From lands of snows to lands of sun.
>
> O, happy ship,
> To rise and dip,
> With the blue crystal at your lip!
> O, happy crew,
> My heart, with you
> Sails, and sails, and sings anew!
>
> No more, no more
> The worldly shore
> Upbraids me with its loud uproar!
> With dreamful eyes
> My spirit lies
> Under the walls of Paradise!

Our ship is steaming along, assisted by her sails filled with a light breeze from the northeast. Her sails consist of a foresail or spenser, gaff-top sail, fore-stay sail, jib, main-stay sail, and maintop-mast-stay sail.

Captain Hess has just told me that we now begin to feel the trade-winds. He detects them by the long gentle swell coming toward us from the southeast, and by the light fleecy clouds off to the east and southeast. These trade-winds sometimes develop into a first-class hurricane, but not usually at this season of the year. May we be spared—for in my enthusiasm for ocean experience I think I will draw the line at hurricanes!

CHAPTER IV.

ON THE CARIBBEAN SEA.

"Behold the sea,
The opaline, the plentiful and strong,
Yet beautiful as is the rose in June,
Fresh as the dewy rainbow in July;
Sea full of food, the nourisher of kinds;
Purger of earth, and medicine of men!"

CAN I ever forget those beautiful days and magnificent nights on the Caribbean Sea! By the time that we entered it, through the Mona Passage, we had all become as well acquainted as if we had been neighbors for years. The *dolce far niente* of an ocean voyage, over a lovely summer sea, is to me the most delightful experience to be had in this sublunary sphere. On such a voyage every one appears at his best. The invigorating air seems not only to fill the lungs with a new lease of life, and the whole body with a keen physical enjoyment, but also fills the heart with good impulses and kindly feelings toward those around you. It inspires you with noble thoughts and takes away, at least for the nonce, all selfishness, all pride, all animosity—and you thank God that you are one of His creatures and have the faculty of thought, and can enjoy His beautiful ocean, not only with two or three of your five senses, but with your soul! Such is the broad, beneficent influence of the ocean! It exhilarates, it sharpens the appetite, it makes you feel young again, and strong, and amiable, and honest, and loving, and a little religious withal!

We watched the sun as it went down into the sea, bathed in a splendor impossible to imitate on canvas or describe with language. Not less beautiful is the glorious rising of the great orb in the sweet cool morning, and he who would not leave his state-room to witness this entrancing sight, is like the man who, unmoved by music and the concord of sweet sounds, is not to be trusted, but is fit only for treason, stratagem and spoils.

One night as we sat on the deck, watching the moonbeams as they played over the quiet sea, a sweet voice, that we had all learned to love, sang to us that exquisite "Evening Song to the Virgin." We had even before this been rather quiet, for the scene was one that inspired thought and repressed conversation—and now this sweet hymn, with its holy sentiment so appropriate to such an hour, made a deep impression on all who heard it, and as we separated for the night, very quietly, it seemed as if the "Adieus" and "Good-nights" were given with a heartiness that bespoke a deeper feeling than the ordinary parting word betrays.

EVENING SONG TO THE VIRGIN.

"*Ave sanctissima*, we lift our souls to thee;
Ora pro nobis, 'tis nightfall on the sea.
   Watch us while shadows lie
    Far o'er the water spread,
   Hear the heart's lonely sigh,
    Thine, too, hath bled.
   Thou that hast looked on death,
    Aid us when death is near;
   Whisper of heav'n to faith,
    Sweet Mother, sweet Mother, hear!
Ora pro nobis, the waves must rock our sleep,
Ora, Mater, ora, Star of the deep!

> "*Ave sanctissima*, we lift our souls to thee;
> *Ora pro nobis*, 'tis nightfall on the sea.
>   Oh, thou whose virtues shine
>   With brightest purity,
>   Come, and each thought refine,
>   Till pure like thee.
>   Oh, save our souls from ill;
>   Guard thou our lives from fear;
>   Our hearts with pleasure fill:
>   Sweet Mother, sweet Mother, hear.
> *Ora pro nobis*, the waves must rock our sleep,
> *Ora, Mater, ora*, Star of the deep!"

I seldom retired to my state-room before midnight. I preferred rather to pace the deck with one of the officers, or lolling back in my steamer chair and gazing upon the waters—sometimes silvery in the radiance of the moon, and at other times gleaming and shining with a phosphorescent light—give rein to my thoughts. Ah, true as the needle to the pole did they always turn lovingly to my native land, and to that one little spot in the great world that is known and cherished by all loving hearts under the sweet appellation of Home.

When the Sun Sinks to Rest.

> "When the sun sinks to rest,
>   And the star of the west
> Sheds its soft silver light o'er the sea;
>   What sweet thoughts arise,
>   As the dim twilight dies—
> For then I am thinking of thee!

> "Oh! then crowding fast
>   Come the joys of the past,
> Through the dimness of days long gone by,
>   Like the stars peeping out,
>   Through the darkness about,
> From the soft silent depth of the sky.

> "And thus, as the night
> Grows more lovely and bright
> With the clustering of planet and star,
> So this darkness of mine
> Wins a radiance divine
> From the light that still lingers afar.
>
> "Then welcome the night,
> With its soft holy light!
> In its silence my heart is more free
> The rude world to forget,
> Where no pleasure I've met
> Since the hour that I parted from thee."

But I must relate a little yarn that was reeled off to me on one of those nights on the Caribbean Sea:

A Thrilling Experience.

"A few years ago," said Mr. Wilkinson, our first officer, "when I was first mate of the bark 'Scud,' on a voyage from Philadelphia to La Guayra, we were sailing along about three knots an hour one very dark night in the Caribbean Sea, within seventy-five or eighty miles of the Venezuelan coast. The weather had been wet and nasty, and there was quite a sea running. The captain said he guessed he would go below, and I went down with him to light my pipe to keep me company during my watch. As I returned on deck I put my two hands out on the rail, which was a very low one, not over sixteen inches high, to peer out into the darkness. Coming out from the light of the cabin to the inky blackness of the night, I thought I saw a light off to the leeward. I took my hands off the rail and drew back to take my pipe out of my mouth to take another look from a standing position. Seeing nothing I stretched my hands to the rail to resume my former position. The bark at that moment gave a sudden lurch and my hands, instead of grasping the rail, went over it, and, my feet slipping on the wet deck at the same moment, I was in the twinkling of an eye plunged into the sea! As soon as I came to the surface I yelled with all my might, 'Throw me a rope.' Fortunately the man at the wheel heard me, and putting the helm hard down, threw the bark up into the wind. As she forged by me the 'bumbkin,' a short spar over the quarter to which the main braces are led, pitched, in the rolling of the vessel, so near me that I grabbed at it, but only touched it with my fingers. I now thought quick as a flash of a new cod line that I had baited with a white rag and thrown over during the afternoon with the hope of catching a fish. I said to myself, 'Old boy, that is your only chance,' and struck out across the wake of the vessel, throwing my arms out in the hope of finding that line. Sure enough I struck it, but not with my hands but with my neck, and grasping it I again hallooed for a rope. In a minute more I felt a rope floating against me, and, taking two or three turns of it around my body under my arms, I sang out, 'Haul in.' This they did with a will, and soon I was safe again on the deck of the bark.

"The captain's nerves were completely unstrung, and as he put his hands over my shoulders in a sort of an embrace, he said, 'My God, Wilkinson, if we had lost you how could I have ever gone home and told your old woman?'

"Yes, that was a close call, and my danger of drowning was no greater than that of being killed by one of the man-eating sharks of which the Caribbean Sea is full."

CHAPTER V.

THE ISLAND OF CURACAO.

AT noon, March 8th, the tropical island of Curacao was plainly in sight, and our captain assured us that we should enter the harbor before sunset. The rugged coasts are eagerly scanned through our spy-glasses, and about four o'clock, when we are within five miles of the harbor, our attention is directed to the extensive phosphate works of an English company on the coast side of a mountain. Ninety-seven per cent. of the mountain is phosphate of lime, and the company has made a great deal of money in mining and exporting it. They pay a royalty to the Dutch government on the production, amounting to over $200,000 per year. Their dock, and harbor, and buildings, and vessels, and the tramway up the side of the mountain, are plainly seen as we steam along the coast.

A little further on we have a fine view of an old Spanish castle on the cliffs on a bay called Curacao Bay, or "Spanish Water," at the mouth of one of the beautiful lagoons with which this island abounds. This castle was built by the Spaniards in the year 1527.

But before we enter the harbor, a few facts concerning the history of Curacoa would seem to be the proper thing to relate, but as statistics are invariably stupid, I will endeavor to give the necessary data as briefly as possible.

The island was discovered in 1499 by Alonzo de Ojeda and Americus Vespucius. It was held by the Spanish from 1527

THE ROUND TOWER, CURACAO.

REMAINS OF AN OLD SPANISH CASTLE. MODERN QUARANTINE BUILDINGS ERECTED NEAR BY.

to 1634, when it was taken from them by the Dutch. It is said that when discovered (and afterward settled) by the Spaniards, the island was inhabited by a race of Indians so noble in stature that they were called giants, all being over six feet, and many seven feet tall. But they were heathen and cannibals, and the Spaniards, with their usual happy blending of religion and murder, proceeded to conquer and convert, and after making them kiss the true cross, they massacred them without delay, thus simultaneously punishing them for eating human flesh, and sending them joyfully to heaven. It is two hundred and fifty-seven years since the bloody flag of Spain waved over the fair island of Curacao, but she left her religious imprint there, and to-day, of the twenty-seven thousand inhabitants, more than twenty thousand are of the Roman Catholic faith.

Then the island was held by the Dutch till the latter part of the eighteenth century, when it was captured by the British, was restored to Holland in 1802, again seized by England in 1807, and finally given up to the Dutch in 1816, by whom it is now held and governed.

It is situated in the Caribbean Sea, about forty-two miles from the north coast of Venezuela, and is about forty-one miles long and from three to seven miles broad. It is not of volcanic origin, but, judging by its formation and other circumstances, the theory is that it formerly was part of the South American main-land. The exports of Curacao are phosphate of lime, salt, divi-divi, orange peel, wool, hides, skins, aloes and peanuts. Its population is about 27,000—7,000 white and 20,000 colored and black. The religious proclivities of its inhabitants are exhibited by 20,000 professing the Roman Catholic faith, 4,500 adhering to the Reformed Church of Holland, and 2,500 worshiping under the old Mosaic form. This, perhaps, is sufficient to relate of its past history, size, exports, population and religion, and what further I will have to say of the island will be a relation of my experience while there, and a few desultory remarks on the impressions received by what I saw and heard.

There are but two licensed pilots at Curacao, one a tall, venerable old man, with a long white beard, and the other a coal-black negro. The white man boarded our steamer and took us through the narrow entrance of the harbor, and, while we remained in Curacao, I could not help noticing that even here, where the colored race far outnumber the white, the Caucasian still holds the "bulge" on his darker brother, for the white pilot was constantly taking in and out the big steamers, while the other had to be content with the lesser crafts and smaller fees.

On either side of the entrance to the harbor are the frowning forts, named, respectively, Fort Amsterdam and Fort Rif, both built by the Dutch about the year 1635. To speak of a fort without prefixing the adjective "frowning" would be in bad form, but the "frown" that these two poor feeble old relics of the 17th century assume in this age of heavy ordnance is laughable, indeed. But they are picturesque, and also useful to a certain degree, because they furnish a sort of a home and employment to a few hundred comically-dressed and stupid-looking Dutch soldiers, and there is a gun somewhere in one of them that is fired off at sunrise, at noon, at sunset, and at eight o'clock in the evening. Yes, and that gun is also fired off "semi-occasionally" to celebrate and give publicity to another event of great importance to these islanders. Can you guess what it is? As I am sure you cannot, I will not keep you in suspense, but tell you at once that it is discharged whenever the *mail* is distributed and ready to be delivered! It reminded me of a time when I lived in a town in Indiana, on the Wabash, where the whole population had

ENTRANCE TO HARBOR OF CURACAO.

the "fever and ague" so bad that the town bell was rung daily at stated intervals for everybody to take quinine!

Adjoining the fort on the right as you enter (which is Fort Amsterdam) is the citadel, which is quite extensive in earthworks, and having a large parade-ground, around which are the barracks. The governor's palace is also located here. It is a large, handsome structure, with inviting looking balconies, and plenty of trees and shrubbery and blooming flowers all about it. Quite a show of military is constantly kept up, and the guards are to be seen in every direction in and around the fort and the governor's palace. A more innocent and peaceful-looking lot of soldiers, however, I never saw, and I offered to bet a box of cigars with one of my fellow-travelers that none of their guns were loaded.

The harbor is a lagoon, not more than three or four hundred feet wide, and extends into the island about three-quarters of a mile or so, where it widens and forms an extensive lake called the "Schattegat." The tide ebbs and flows all through this deep lagoon into the Schattegat, and there is plenty of water for several miles up into the interior of the island for the largest vessels in the world. While the whole of this lagoon (for the lake and all is but a lagoon) may properly be called the harbor of Curacao, and a most completely landlocked one it is, yet the narrow part of it, extending from Forts Amsterdam and Rif, to where it widens into the Schattegat, a distance, I believe, of not over a mile, is the only part that is used as the harbor. Here, on either side, the steamers and vessels can come right up to the wharves.

The harbor divides the town in two. The east side is in three divisions, called, respectively, "Wilhelmstadt," named after one of the five princes of Orange, "Pietermaay" and "Scharlo." Across the lagoon is called "Otrabanda," which means "other side," and here our steamer came to her wharf.

THE HARBOR OF CURACAO.

The chief business part of the city is Wilhelmstadt, that being where all the principal stores are located. The other three divisions are mostly given up to residences, churches, and warehouses along the docks. All sections of the place present very pleasing pictures, the houses being substantially built of brick and stone and stuccoed, and all painted yellow

A CURACAO FERRYMAN.

with white trimmings, and with bright red tile roofs. All the buildings look very old, and some, being of the Moorish style of architecture, doubtless date back to the 16th century, when the Spaniards had a thriving colony here.

I have never been to Holland, but those who have, and have been to Curacao also, say that it resembles, very strongly, the

Dutch towns on the Zuyder Zee. Perhaps one-third of the population reside in Otrabanda, and, consequently, the ferry business between there and Wilhelmstadt, Pietermaay and Scharlo, across the harbor, is quite lively. It is carried on by one hundred and fifty-six licensed and numbered flat-boats, each propelled by one-man power. The colored skipper sculls the boat with a heavy-bladed oar, leaning his forehead hard against the end of it, as, with his hands and arms, he gives it the necessary motion. This is *sculling* in a double sense, and the dullest wit who ever goes over this "Twickenham" ferry never fails to remark that there is a good deal of *head-work* about the business. The ferriage is five Dutch coppers, about two cents of our money, but if you hand out a small piece of silver you get no change any more than you do at the candy or flower booth of a church fair. They can't understand English *at all* when change is needed, and we soon learned the racket and kept ourselves supplied with an abundance of the small copper coins of the realm. And this leads me to remark that the language spoken in Curacao is a mixture of Dutch, Spanish and Portuguese, with a little English thrown in for seasoning. It makes a very peculiar dialect, and is called *papiamento*. To hear it gabbled by the negroes and negresses, as they laugh and flirt by the water-side, you come to the conclusion that the meaning of *papiamento* is Irish stew or boarding-house hash — a little of everything. But the business men, who, by the way, are largely made up of Jews, nearly all speak English, and know how to drive a shrewd bargain in a language and a style that you thoroughly understand. The streets are mostly very narrow ones, like the streets of all southern or tropical towns and cities first settled by the Spaniards. I have often speculated on the reason for this, for there must have been a reason. If it was for greater shade and a cooler atmosphere, I think the benefit gained in this regard is more than overbalanced by the increased filthiness of the narrow passages — too greatly honored to be called streets — and the difficulty of getting enough of heaven's fresh air into them to carry off the vile odors.

While there are a fair number of pretty good stores in

THEY CARRY THEIR BURDENS ON THEIR HEADS
AND NONE IN THEIR HEARTS. CURACAO.

Wilhelmstadt, carrying rather large stocks, there are innumerable little shops, the excessive smallness of which you can scarcely imagine. For instance, I saw a shoe-shop, four feet wide by eight feet long, with four men at work in it, and a tailor-shop, next door, perhaps a foot or two larger, with six men working in it! Every doorway is a store-room for a half-dressed negro woman to display, for sale, her trays and baskets of sweetmeats, vegetables, etc. All the negro women carry their burdens on their heads. They evidently have none to carry in their hearts, like thousands of their fairer and more enlightened sisters, and they go laughing and talking along,

THE AIRY FAIRY LILIAN, WHO WASHED
MY LINEN. CURACAO.

without apparently giving a single thought to the tray, or tub, or pail, or basket, or bundle so nicely balanced on their head.

The harbor and the sea is the general wash-tub for the lower classes. Here they wash their clothes, laying them on the rocks and beating them with a club, and, after rinsing and wringing, they replace them in the tub, and, balancing it on their head, march off to the hill-side to spread them out to dry. I do not think they understand the intricate modern invention of a clothes-line, and I would not, for the world, disturb their sweet and simple contentment by an innovation such as that. I had three new linen shirts soaked in the harbor, beaten with a club (I was not wearing them at the time), and dried on a cactus bush, and, though bearing plenty of evidence of the fearful ordeal, they will do to wear around home, I fondly hope, for several weeks yet!

The negro women all wear turbans on their heads, and they don't seem to care about the color, "so long as it is red." Their costume consists of but one other garment, and this is a light calico dress, made *en train*. In front it is quite short, displaying, in bold relief, their bare feet and ankles, but to have it trail behind seems to be the inexorable law of colored fashion in Curacao.

The negro children, from one to five years of age, toddle about in pure innocence, clothed only in the simplicity of Nature, which may be said to cover them as with a garment, only the garment is *non est*.

The living of these ignorant negroes is about as simple as their dress. Those who propel the ferry-boats sleep in them and eat the simple articles that are peddled about by the negro women, who carry them in trays on their heads. Those who keep house do so in the most primitive manner, in tenement houses that appeared to be crowded with occupants. Their rooms have scarcely any furniture, and what there is seems to have been in use for many generations past. The drinking habit prevails, to a great extent, and I was told that these poor ignorant creatures spend all their money (except what is absolutely necessary for food and a trifle of clothing) for intoxicating liquors.

In reflecting on the degraded condition of these negro laborers of Curacao, I am reminded of some of the utterances of that noble champion of Labor in the United States, T. V. Powderly, General Master Workman of the Order of Knights of Labor. He strikes at the root of the whole trouble amongst the laboring classes when he declares that "*ignorance* and *intemperance* are the twin evils that keep the working classes

ENTICED INTO THE PHOTOGRAPHER'S ROOM.
CURACAO.

in poverty, and at which he intends to strike the hardest blows of which he is capable." Again, he says, and I wish it could be posted in every factory and workshop throughout the land: "I will oppose no reform or reformer, but will seek to aid their legitimate efforts by battling for the education of the children of the land; by protesting against the spending of the hard earnings of labor in the saloon and brothel. Ignorance begets intemperance, intemperance turns freemen into slaves; slavery begets monopoly, monopoly bribes congresses and legislatures, throttles justice by bribing the courts, and begets anarchy. Strike a telling blow at anarchy, monopoly, slavery and intemperance by killing ignorance in the school-room. Let us demand the compulsory education of American youth."

The manufactures of Curacao amount to but little. A pretty sort of jewelry is made of gold obtained at Aruba, an island near by. Some neat little work-boxes and small writing-desks are also made of mahogany.

As Curacao is, practically, a free port, there being but one and a half per cent. duty on imports, all European goods can be obtained cheaper there than in the United States.

CHAPTER VI.

CURACAO.

THERE are a great many small vessels sailing between here and the various sea-ports of Venezuela. The thirty per cent. duty charged by the Venezuelan government on all imports (except machinery, which is free) is a great temptation and incentive to smuggle goods from Curacao to that coast, and I learned that smuggling is carried on very largely by means of these small, fast-sailing schooners that are seen in the harbor.

In the old days of two or three centuries ago, this island was one of the favorite lurking-places of the pirates of the Spanish Main. Here, in these deep lagoons, sheltered from storms and entirely hidden from view by the hills and cliffs, they lay in wait for the rich Spanish galleon laden with the gold of the Incas, or the almost equally richly-laden merchantmen with wine and silks, in the Caribbean Sea, and when sighted they gave chase, and seldom did their prey escape. Seldom, also, did they take any prisoners. They killed all, plundered the vessels and then burned them. They fought hard, lived luxuriously, and died with their boots on. But they were all religious! They had their priests and their chapels, gave largely to the Mother Church, and always kept their religious accounts square to date! But the gay and festive pirate and the bold buccaneer of the Spanish Main sail these beautiful seas no more. Some of their golden plunder is said to be still buried in the island of Curacao, but the actors

BROAD STREET, CURACAO.

are gone, and if their spirits ever revisit the scenes of their former revelry and fierce combats, they disturb not the peaceful, quiet and contented minds of these happy islanders. Only the sneaking smuggler remains to remind one of those old days when all the islands and the waters of the Spanish Main were the paradise of violent men, engaged in unlawful business, and hesitating not to do murder and every other sin of the decalogue for the sake of gold.

But to return to Curacao. I had letters of introduction to prominent citizens there from Morris Coster, Esq., editor and publisher of the New Amsterdam *Gazette*, among them one to Hon. J. H. W. Gravenhorst, late Governor of the islands of Buen Ayer and Aruba, two of the Dutch West India possessions. I found the governor a very intelligent and hale and hearty gentleman of from fifty-five to sixty years of age, residing with his family in a finely located mansion overlooking the harbor. A more hospitable reception from the governor and his excellent wife I never had accorded to me by any one, and I was immediately made to feel perfectly at home. The governor's children are all grown up. Two of his daughters are married; one of them, Mrs. Forbes, with her husband, E. H. S. B. Forbes, a very genial and well-informed man, resides with her father, as does also an unmarried daughter and a son. My first visit to this delightful home was the second evening after our arrival at Curacao. I took with me Signor Rudloff and Mr. Angell, and to this day I am tormented with the thought that to Signor Rudloff's fluency in German and Spanish, and to young Angell's good looks and glib tongue, I was more indebted for my cordial reception and subsequent attentions, than to my own substantial worth and thoroughly gentlemanly appearance — especially with the female portion of the household! But 'tis ever thus, the sweetest roses of life have some thorn that rankles, and the bosom of either man

U. S. CONSUL SMITH'S STEAM YACHT, "RELIANCE," IN THE LAGOON AT CURACAO.

or woman is always tortured with some tinge of jealousy or disappointed hopes!

Another kind letter from a New York friend introduced me to Captain L. B. Smith, the United States Consul at Curacao. Captain Smith is from Maine, has lived here eleven years, and does a large business in ice and lumber which he brings in his own vessels from his native state. He generously placed at my disposal his beautiful little steam yacht, managed by his son, a very pleasant and intelligent young man of twenty-one. The yacht cost two thousand dollars, and I spent so many pleasant hours in her that I had a photograph taken, and by the engraver's art I am enabled to give a picture of her as she appeared in the lagoon at the foot of the small mountain called "Sublica," on the top of which is built Fort Nassau. This fort is garrisoned by about fifty Dutch soldiers, and is used also as a signal station. Signals displayed on a flag-pole make known to the citizens of Curacao the approach of vessels, and designate particularly by the various numbers and positions of the flags just what kind of a vessel or steamer draws near the sacred soil.

I invited the Gravenhorst family and the three "bug-hunters" to accompany me one morning on an excursion in the steam launch up the lagoon into the Schattegat. We started about seven o'clock, after partaking of a cup of fragrant Maracaibo coffee at the governor's mansion, intending to return at the usual breakfast hour of eleven. The evening before, as we sat on the governor's piazza, sipping our tea, we had been pressed to visit the estate of J. H. B. Gravenhorst (a cousin of the governor's) five miles in the country, and, as we recalled this invitation, our young skipper said he could land us within ten-minute's walk of his plantation. So thither we sped over the clear and tranquil waters of this lovely ocean lake. Soon we reached the little dock, and, disembarking, we walked

4

slowly up a beautifully shaded lane to "our cousin's" plantation, which has the name of "Gasparito." Here we were met by cousin J. H. B. and his wife and daughter, and escorted up the wide stone steps to the spacious stone veranda where *ten* large cane rocking-chairs awaited our occupancy!

The ten-minute walk had moistened the epidermis of my two hundred and twenty-five advoirdupois to such an extent that a large cane rocker, a palmetto fan, a glass of cool lemonade and a strong cigar seemed just what my frail tenement of flesh required. Inspiration, or long experience in ministering to the wants of visitors from a Northern clime, led our kind host to provide just these very articles, and I noticed that our "lean and hungry" bug-hunters took very kindly to the rest, the zephyr, the refreshment, and the solace afforded by these important factors in the comfort of mankind in West India climate—the chair, the fan, the lemonade and the cigar.

The view from this piazza was lovely indeed, and the governor told me that he never sat there gazing on the beautiful panorama spread out before him without feeling like "dropping into poetry," like Silas Wegg; but he had thus far resisted the strong temptation, and had contented himself with making pencil sketches of the exquisite land and waterscape.

In the conservatory of this hospitable abode we were shown a great variety of tropical plants and flowers. Many of them were growing in boxes, on the ends of which we read in plain English the familiar legend, "Premium Safety Oil, 150° Fire Test."

In the garden we saw the tamarind tree, and, also, the saddle tree, any slip of which will grow if inserted in the soil, and many other trees and shrubs strange to Northern eyes. The fleet-footed and sharp-eyed lizards darted about in every direction in the grass, and, to the great joy of the entomologists, three new varieties of beetles were captured and presented to Mr. Angell.

Curacao is certainly a fine winter resort—an El Dorado for invalids. As every Spanish name has some significant meaning, I was not at all surprised to learn that Curacao means "healing." When in Florida, a year or two ago, I was greatly amused at the persistency with which the residents of every bog-hole village asserted, "There is no *malaria* here," when it stalks all up and down that much-advertised and overrated land, like the "sheeted dead that did squeak and gibber in the streets of Rome."

But here in Curacao (pronounced, as I have before remarked, "Cure-a-so") the very name of malaria is unknown, or, to distort the words of Bulwer, " In the bright lexicon of Curacao there is no such word as malaria."

I should like to see that fine old mansion on the Estado Gasparito enlarged and turned into a hotel for the accommodation of visitors from the North, and though I have no weak lungs to be healed, I should like to engage that piazza for my abiding-place during the months of February and March of every winter. This house was built by a Spanish nobleman in the 16th century. It is constructed of sandstone and coral, and stuccoed with water-lime. Its present owner keeps it in excellent repair, and it has every appearance of being good for several more centuries.

There is a beverage much prized by *bon vivants*, called "Curacao *liqueur*." Of course, *you and I* (who "never drink") care nothing about this famous decoction, and the mere mention of it is forced upon *me*, in my keen desire to be a faithful chronicler of all that I can recollect that pertains to the history or the traditions of this beautiful isle of the sea. Know, then, that "Curacao *liqueur*," though made in large quantities, and, alas, as I fear, drunk also in large quantities, is not, and never was, made in Curacao! It is distilled in Holland only, and takes its name simply from the aromatic flavor given to it by the *peel* of an orange indigenous to the soil of Curacao. This orange, which is not good to eat, but the *peel* of which is so highly prized by distillers in Holland, is cultivated by mine host Gravenhorst on his plantation Gasparito. The *peel*, only, is exported, and Mr. G. derives a large income from this peculiar, though, to our mind, slightly reprehensible crop! So when you are offered a glass of Curacao *liqueur* (of course, as a medicine only), you will remember this interesting fact which I have told to you regarding the derivation of its name. *Honi soit qui mal y pense!*

But the " foot of Time," which " travels in divers paces with divers persons," was "swift," with us, and we were admonished by our young captain that if we would reach our steamer at the breakfast hour we must take our departure. Reluctantly the farewells were said, and we left that lovely island home, sincerely regretting our visit there had necessarily been so short. Before returning to the dock, we made the entire circuit of the Schattegat. At various points we saw beautiful country-seats, nearly all of which had pretty names like " Pareda," and " Bleinheim," but one had the scriptural name of Mt. Ararat! We reached the steamer Philadelphia at precisely eleven o'clock, full of enthusiasm (equaled only by our appetites), and joined our genial Captain Hess in doing full justice to a breakfast at which some fine fresh fish formed a prominent part.

At noon of this eventful day we had to say good-by to Mr. Logan, who took a small steamer to Maracaibo. It was with sorrow that we parted with one of our trio of bug-hunters. We had held a strong hand all the voyage, for "three of a kind beats two pairs," but now we have but a single pair and our spirits are depressed. We pass, and throw up our hand!

The good people of Curacao have but few amusements, such as concerts, theatrical entertainments, and the like, but they

STREET IN PIETERMAAY, CURACAO.

are strong in clubs. In company with Consul Smith, we visited " Gechazelhead " Club, in Wilhelmstadt, and staid an hour in its pleasant parlors. I have spelled the name of this club as I caught it by word of mouth, but, upon further thought and research, I am rather inclined to think that the word is " Gezeligheid," and means " sociability." If you have any loose or false teeth, I would not advise you to try to pronounce it. I noticed that Captain Smith looked as if he was suffering from a slight paralytic stroke after he gave it to me.

There was a tidal wave September 23, 1877, which damaged the town of Wilhelmstadt to the amount of six hundred thousand dollars. This estimate, however, I believe includes the loss of two or three small vessels, which were driven out to sea and never heard from afterward. The ruin wrought by this mighty wave can still be partially seen, although many of the houses destroyed have since been rebuilt. My friend, Mr. Forbes, was one of the victims of this terrible visitation of the hurricane and tidal wave. His house was completely wrecked, and he and his wife escaped from it but a few moments before it fell in ruins. A previous storm, on the 24th of June, 1831, raged with great violence on the island and caused severe damage, but to the adjacent islands of Buen Ayer and Aruba it was of a more serious nature than to Curacao.

There are so many interesting things to tell about this island that I find I must omit many, or I shall prolong this narrative to an unpardonable length. But I cannot avoid relating here a bit of biography given me by Governor Gravenhorst, as he pointed out to me the spot where had, until recently, lain the remains of one of the heroes of the South American War of Independence.

Admiral Louis Brion was born in Curacao, July 6, 1782, and was educated in Amsterdam. He returned from Holland to this island in 1799, and, obtaining the rank of captain in the militia here, he served in 1804 against the English, under command of Commodore Murry, who were entrenched on the mountian called "Kabrutenberg," in the neighborhood of Fort Beckenberg, which he attacked with but one hundred and sixty men, and after a most desperate battle put the English to flight.

Afterward, under the renowned General Simon Bolivar, known as the Liberator of South America, he fought with great bravery, and for his eminent services in these wars of independence, not only as a soldier, but in bringing stores and arms from London, in his own vessels, for the republican forces, in their prolonged and patriotic struggle against the Spanish tyranny, he was created admiral. It is said that he studied navigation in the United States.

His career was characterized by great bravery and skill in handling his fleet of gun-boats, in his numerous engagements with the Spanish men-of-war; but he did not live to see the Spaniards dispossessed of the country that they had so long ruled over and plundered. He returned from South America to Curacao in 1821, and died there the twenty-first of September, the same year, and was buried at "Rosentak," near the country seat of Gasparito. In September, 1881, just sixty years after his death, his ashes were disinterred by order of Guzman Blanco, the President of Venezuela, and conveyed with great pomp and ceremony to Caracas, where they now lie with the ashes of many other South American heroes, in the Pantheon in that city.

Mine host of Gasparito, Mr. J. H. B. Gravenhorst, witnessed the disinterment of the ashes of this illustrious man, and inspired by the interesting occasion wrote some verses, in Dutch, to the memory of Admiral Brion, a printed copy of which was given me by the governor. They have been translated for me by Rev. William Hall, of New York, and I take pleasure in giving both the original and the translation:

Eenige Regels

Toegewyd aan de nagedachtenis van den ADMIRAAL LOUIS BRION *by de opdelving van zyn staffelyk overschot te Curacao op den 17den September, 1881.*

Niet langer hier vertoefd, niet langer hier gerust
Vergeten, onbekend, door niemand hier beweend ;
Men roept U op, BRION ; daar ginds op d'overkust
Eischt men Uw dierbaar stof, vraagt men om Uw gebeent' ;
U dan voor 't laatst gedankt, nogmaals voor U gerouwd.
Columbia ! gy wilt BRION, uw' redder, eeren ;
't Is of zyn droeve schim my by zyn graf weêrhoudt
En my van tranen spreekt, van bloed en overheeren
Van Venezuela's volk, in ketens eens geslagen,
Van koningen beroofd van troon, van land en goed ;
Van misdaad, wanhoop, duldeloos lyden, plagen,
Van ongekende wreedheid, dorst naar goud en bloed ;
't Is of zyn vlammend oog, waarvoor Castilië beefde
Nog vol ontroering staart op wreede folteringen
En of de fiere held, die steeds naar vryheid streefde,
De lage beulen wil in yz'ren kluisters wringen.
't Is of zyn mond nog vloekt de snoode Castilianen
En van het leed verhaalt, door hen alom verwekt.
Columbia ! besproeid met zooveel bloed en tranen,
Vereeuwig thans BRION, zyn roem is onbevlekt ;
Begroet den eed'len held, die uit Uw schoone staten
Den vyand heeft verjaagd, zyn legers heeft verslagen ;
Vergood, bemin den held, die niet heeft toegelaten,
Dat gy, als slaaf, verguisd, het Spaansche juk zoudt dragen ;
Bezing den fieren leeuw, die aan Uw oosterstranden
De Spaansche vloot verwon, verbrand heeft en vernield ;
Bazuin zyn deugden rond, verhaal aan alle landen,
Dat gy, Columbia ! weent by zyn graf geknield.

—*J. H. B. Gravenhorst.*

Lines,

To the Memory of ADMIRAL LOUIS BRION, *on the Occasion of the Removal of his Remains, Interred at Curacao, September 17th, 1881. By the Hon. J. H. B. Gravenhorst. Printed in Wilhelmstadt, Curacao.*

No longer here detained, no longer here to rest,
Forgotten, unknown, by no one here deplored,
They call thee up, Brion ! and everywhere on yonder coast.
They ask for thy dear dust, thy buried form ;
Thou now, at last art thanked, anew art wept.

THIRTY DAYS ON THE CARIBBEAN. 57

> Columbia! thy Liberator, Brion, thou wilt honor;
> 'T is he, or his sad shade, me by his tomb doth hold,
> To me doth speak of tears, of blood and tyrants,
> Of Venezuela's folk, in chains once stricken,
> By crime, despair, pains intolerable, plagues,
> By cruelties unknowable, thirst for gold and blood;
> 'T is he, or his flaming eye, 'fore which Castilia trembled,
> Still full of terror, just fruit of persecutions dire,
> As if the fiery hero whoe'er for freedom strove,
> Might yet the base hangmen in iron fetters wring;
> 'T is he, or his voice, that curseth still Spain's sordid sons,
> And of the suffering telleth, through the universe resounded.
> Columbia! besmeared with blood and tears,
> Now immortalize thy Brion—unspotted glory his!
> Salute thy noble champion, who from your beauteous States
> The foe hath driven, his legions smitten;
> Repay with love the man heroic, who ne'er could brook
> That thou enslaved, deceived, should wear Castilian yoke:
> And laud the lion bold, who on yon eastern strands,
> Vanquished Hispania's fleet, burned and destroyed;
> Trumpet his virtues, to every land proclaim
> That thou, Columbia, kneeling, dost with tears his grave bedew.

Slavery previously existed in Curacao, but was done away with July 1, 1863, about the time the shackles fell off from our own four millions of bondmen and women.

The Holland Government paid to the owners eighty dollars each for every slave emancipated, which was satisfactory to all concerned, and now the blacks work for from twelve cents a day in the salt vats, to twenty or thirty cents a day in other employments requiring physical strength but no particular amount of brains. A master-carpenter or mason receives sixty cents a day, while the journeyman jogs along happily through this mundame sphere entirely satisfied with the pecuniary recompense of forty cents per diem for his labor.

A diligent inquiry could discover no Knights of Labor organization on the island, and "strikes" are unknown. Whether a different state of affairs, such as the K. of L. organization would inaugurate, would improve the present condition of these 20,000 negroes, is a question that I leave open to those who care to ponder upon it. If they could be weaned from guzzling gin, and other injurious and unnatural beverages, it would probably be of greater benefit to them than an increase of wages; for with them more money means more gin.

A NEGLECTED OPPORTUNITY.

One evening, at the hospitable residence of ex-Governor Gravenhorst, his son said to me, while we were sipping our tea in the moonlight on the broad stone piazza, "Mr. H., the house that I am with here import the very best quality of Holland gin, and if you want a few bottles to take home with you, I can let you have them at our wholesale prices." Coward that I was, I assumed a grateful look, and, thanking him warmly, said that, perhaps before I left Curacao I would avail myself of his kind offer! What I *ought* to have said would have been about as follows: "Thank you, Mr. Gravenhorst, I never drink gin, or any other beverage of an intoxicating nature. I am opposed to it on principle, believing it to be the greatest as well as the most insidious enemy of mankind. In my own country we are endeavoring to put a stop to the liquor traffic by legislation, and at our last election I voted the entire Prohibition ticket with the exception of the Republican congressional candidate, who is my banker and personal friend." But "'tis conscience makes cowards of us all," and I neglected this most favorable opportunity to implant my temperance sentiments in the breast of this young gentleman!

Ah, how universal is the infatuation in men to put "an enemy in their mouths to steal away their brains!" Self-indulgence in the drinking habit, or some selfish interest, direct or indirect, in the liquor traffic, often leads travelers to report very favorably on the happy state of affairs that they found in this country, or that country, where the peasantry all drank their wine or beer with their wives and children, and were none the worse for it, either in body, mind or estate! But it is all "bosh," and they know it. Every intelligent man who travels with his eyes open and his intellect unclouded to receive honest impressions, knows that there is not a country on the face of the globe, nor an island of the sea, where the use of intoxicating liquors is not the same blasting curse to the human race there, as it is in Massachusetts or Pennsylvania.

> "O, thou invisible spirit of wine,
> If thou hast no name to be known by,
> Let us call thee—devil!"

Fort Beckenberg, which I have just mentioned in connection with the biography of Admiral Brion, is situated on what is known as Caracas Bay, and was built by the Spaniards in 1527. It is now used for quarantine purposes, in connection with other spacious buildings which were erected in 1884 by the Dutch government at an expense of thirty-eight thousand dollars.

All over the island are remains of forts and signal stations, interesting in their history, which remind one of the varying fortunes of war through which this island has passed. But I must hasten on, and before leaving the subject of Curacao, speak of my attendance at church in the ancient religious edifice built within the walls of Fort Amsterdam. In company with Captain Hess, Mr. H. T. Livingston, and Dr. Hutchinson, I entered one of the scull-propelled ferry boats on Sunday morning at nine o'clock, and proceeded to attend church in accordance with the custom of my pious ancestry for many generations. We reached the church a half-hour before the time of service, and were politely shown about the ancient building by a deacon who was an acquaintance of our captain's. The first thing that attracted our attention on the outside was a cannon-ball, inserted apparently with great force in the wall of the church, just above the main entrance. This is a souvenir of the English who placed it there, *nolens volens*, about an hundred years ago, and the agent that did the job was a brass cannon mounted on an eminence across the lagoon, about one mile back of Otrabanda. The English and Dutch were having a little trouble about that time, and the English vessels, not being able to enter the harbor, landed their guns through the surf on the sea-shore, and, planting a battery on a hill, bombarded the town of Wilhelmstadt and Fort Amsterdam to a capitulation.

I forget the date of the erection of the church, but the imprint on the Bible in the pulpit is 1756, but that is probably a new affair in comparison to the church itself. The floor of the church is sanded to the depth of about an inch or so, and is as noiseless to the thickest boots as an Axminster carpet would be. The audience part of the church, exclusive of pulpit and organ-gallery, is about forty feet wide by fifty feet in length. Immediately opposite the pulpit is a high and rather pretentious private box for the governor. The center of the church is seated with ordinary wood-seat chairs, and here the women sit and receive the full force of the discharge from the pulpit, while the men, the greater sinners, sit in pews around the sides of the room and only receive the scattering shot. This is wrong. Perhaps a guilty sense of extreme wickedness, and a consciousness of deserving a thorough overhauling and denunciation from the minister, prompted me to take a seat among the chairs in the center of the church. I took Brother Livingston with me, but Brothers Hess and Hutchinson took the regulation seats for sinful men in the pews.

I noticed that the girls (all terribly homely creatures) tittered as we took our seats, and, divining the cause, I was not at all surprised, when, a few minutes afterward, a square-rigged old

Dutch deacon came and politely requested us to change our seats from the chairs to the pews. At this the thirty-one homely girls (the entire female portion of the congregation) tittered again, and the occurrence seemed to keep them in good spirits all through the session. I congratulated myself upon being the cause of so much unalloyed happiness, and felt for once that my life had not been in vain. As for Brothers Hess and Hutchinson, the looks of mock solemnity and pity which they assumed in the hour of our humiliation was too exasperating for endurance, and I fear that my life may be too short for an opportunity to present itself wherein I can get even with them.

The numbers of the hymns to be sung are painted in large figures on square blocks and hung up on the four massive pillars which support the roof. The organ sounded pretty well and was vigorously played, with considerable squeaking of the keys and noise of the pump, but the singing was droned out in a most depressing manner. Everything was in Dutch, and Brother Livingston and I had to imagine the sentiment contained in the hymns that were sung. Perhaps what impressed me most in this part of the service was the fervor with which Captain Hess entered into it. He held his hymn-book in both hands, up high, and, as he soared away with closed eyes, in a sort of holy ecstacy — on the *wrong note* — I felt more drawn to him than ever from the similarity of our natures and education, both being very much inclined to religion, and, also, to vocal music, and knowing dreadful little about either! The sermon was in two acts. After preaching about half an hour, the good man stopped and gave out a hymn, and I thought what a thoroughly sensible man he was to preach such a short sermon — not too short, you know, but just short enough. But lo! and behold, after the hymn was finished he began to preach again! His text, I had ascertained, was from the chapter that he had read at the commencement of the service — Matthew 25th — containing the parable of the talents, but which verse it was I could not exactly determine. But my accusing conscience supplied it, and I felt sure it must be the one beginning, "Thou wicked and slothful servant," and, as he looked directly at me, it seemed that he said, in substance, "And thou miserable sinner from Pennsylvania, what hast *thou* done with the talent which thy Lord has given thee?" and then he proceeded to rehearse to me my unprofitable life, and, as I winced and trembled under his just denunciations, he gave me a closing home thrust with the question, "Didst thou not promise thy best earthly friend to read a chapter every day from the little red testament that was put in thy satchel, and how hast thou kept that promise?" I dared not look up. I felt sure that the eyes of Hess and Hutchinson were upon me, and that they were saying to themselves, "Ah, now he's catching it," and that the thirty-one homely girls, in their dowdy white dresses and straw hats trimmed with blue ribbons, were gloating over my misery. Never before did I perspire so much as I did under that sermon in Dutch, and I shall long remember, if not profit by, the discourse of the Rev. Dr. Tyderman of Curacao. Judging from the audience assembled at this service, being thirty-one females and eleven males, I conclude that religion in this island is at rather a low ebb. But here, as elsewhere, it holds true that the women worshipers far outnumber those of the sterner sex.

The next morning at five o'clock, young Mr. Arthur B. Smith, son of the American consul, met me by appointment, with a small boat rowed by a negro, and together we made an excursion up a lagoon called "Zackato," the entrance to which is just by Fort Rif at the mouth of the harbor. Along this lagoon are located the general hospital, the marine hospital, the mad-house and the lazaretto. On an eminence about two miles away we could plainly see an old square fort or earthworks, said to have been built in a single night by the English, in the year 1804, when they bombarded Fort Amsterdam and the town of Wilhelmstadt. For a mile or so, this lagoon is wide like a lake, and quite shallow, but afterward it is very narrow and leads winding along for about half a mile to where the old salt beds were made centuries ago by the Spaniards. The bushes along the narrow part of the lagoon held thousands of oysters which were clinging to them, and made a curious sight. The negroes sometimes eat them, but they are not very palatable. We saw numbers of large birds of various kinds, which did not seem to be much afraid of us, and I conclude that but little shooting is done here. On the high grounds were large flocks of goats, the raising of which for milk, and food, and hides, is carried on extensively in the island.

At the old salt beds we landed, and walked a few hundred feet to the shore of the Caribbean Sea. The beach was a perfect mass of coral rocks, or rather fragments of coral, and I gathered a dozen or more beautiful specimens of both the white and pink coral.

The Coral Grove.

Deep in the wave is a Coral Grove,
Where the purple mullet and gold-fish rove,
Where the sea-flower spreads its leaves of blue,
That never are wet with falling dew,
But in bright and changeful beauty shine,
Far down in the green and glassy brine.
 The floor is of sand like the mountain drift,
And the pearl shells spangle the flinty snow;
 From coral rocks the sea-plants lift
Their boughs where the tides and billows flow;
 The water is calm and still below,
For the winds and waves are absent there,
 And the sands are bright as the stars that glow
In the motionless fields of upper air;

There with its waving blade of green,
The sea-flag streams through the silent water,
And the crimson leaf of the dulse is seen
To blush like a banner bathed in slaughter;
There with a light and easy motion
The fan-coral sweeps through the clear deep sea,
And the yellow and scarlet tufts of ocean
Are bending like corn on the upland lea;
And life, in rare and beautiful forms,
Is sporting amid those bowers of stone,
And is safe, when the wrathful spirit of storms
Has made the top of the wave his own;
And when the ship from his fury flies,
Where the myriad voices of ocean roar,
When the wind-god frowns in the murky skies,
And demons are waiting the wreck on shore,
Then far below, in the peaceful sea,
The purple mullet and gold-fish rove,
Where the waters murmur tranquilly
Through the bending twigs of the Coral Grove.

—*James Percival.*

The Caves of Curacao.

There are many caves in this island; but the most interesting is that of Hato, located in a small mountain one hundred and fifty feet high, on the estate "Hato," about three miles from the town, on the north coast of the island. Although the extent of it is not known, it is considered as one of the largest in the island, consisting of many extensive galleries and high arches of stone. The natural formation is sand and limestone. The name "Hato" was given to the estate by the Spaniards. The Caribbean Indians were the discoverers of this and other caves, which were by tradition inhabited by them. As there are no rivers nor brooks in the island, and the Indians having no iron utensils to dig wells, they occupied this estate and others, where they discovered springs to procure them sufficient water. On the estate Hato there is a spring of crystalline water flowing during the whole year from the cave mountain into the

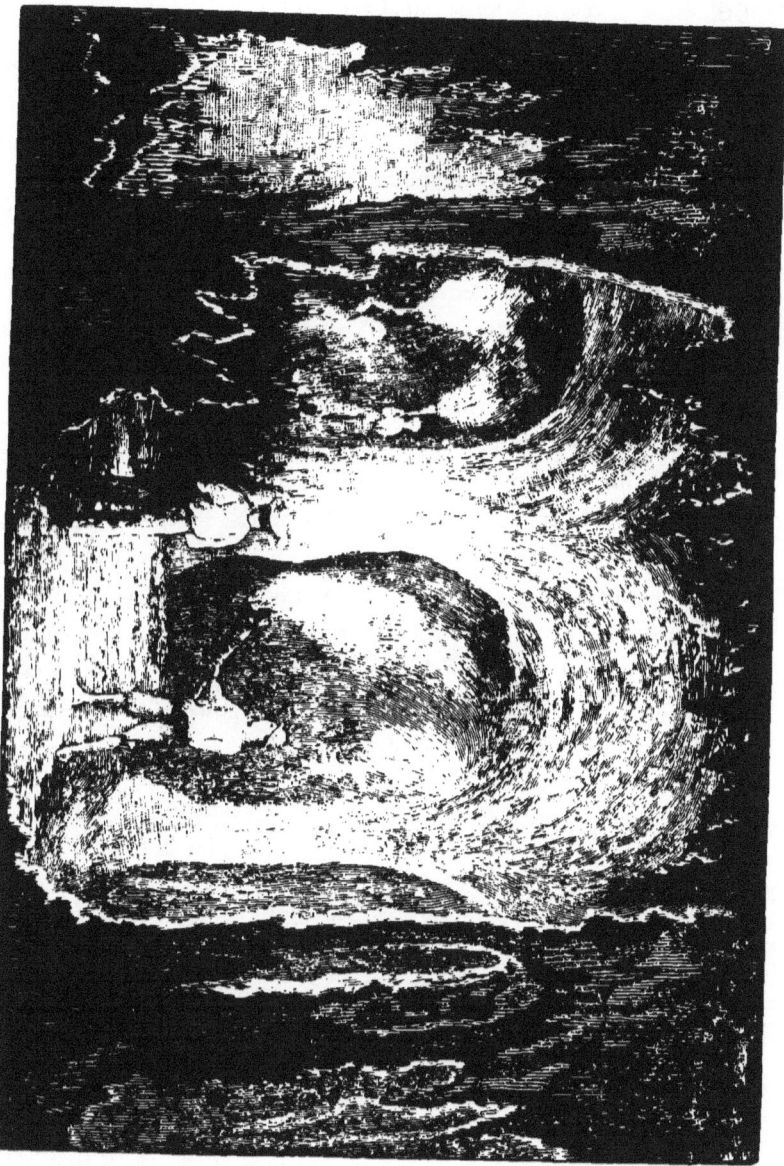

INTERIOR VIEW OF ONE OF THE CHAMBERS IN THE CAVE OF HATO, ISLAND OF CURACOA.

valley, where large reservoirs have been made to keep the water for agricultural and other purposes. This water has proved to be a kind of mineral water, and is of a very good taste, and said to possess medicinal qualities. As I needed no medicine, I but tasted of it, and waited for a good square drink till I returned to the town.

On the estate San Pedro, in the same direction as Hato, but ten miles from the town, there is also a cave and a spring, but of less importance than the former. This is called the Cave of San Pedro.

Our engraving gives a faithful representation of one of the interior chambers of the Cave of Hato. I did not enter the cave, having been entirely satisfied with cave experience in an exhaustive walk of five miles through the "Cuevas de Bellamar," in the island of Cuba, two years ago. I was perfectly willing to accept as true all the marvelous tales of its interior magnificence, and even the tradition that it was the place where all of Captain Kidd's treasures were buried, but respectfully declined to enter its gloomy portals.

CHAPTER VII.

THE SPANISH MAIN.

> "The sea! the sea! the open sea!
> The blue, the fresh, the ever free!
> Without a mark, without a bound,
> It runneth the earth's wide region round;
> It plays with the clouds; it mocks the skies;
> Or like a cradled creature lies."

AND now the time approached when we must bid farewell to the island of Curacao, and proceed on our voyage to Venezuela. Our invalids had improved wonderfully during our sojourn there. Miss N. had been able to take long walks and rides without fatigue, and Mr. Morrison had recovered his voice. That Curacao is a most interesting spot, with a climate near to perfection, was the unanimous verdict. We had found the citizens most hospitable, and the invitations we had received to dinners and to evening parties, were more numerous than we could possibly accept. We made our parting calls on many friends and they in turn came to the steamer to see us off. At six in the evening we steamed out of the harbor and were once more on the bosom of the beautiful sea—that historic sea, taking its name from the Carib Indians and also bearing the title of "The Spanish Main," a title that is surrounded by a halo of romance and adventure, in which brave mariners of all nations, as well as bloody pirates, are mingled.

The night was calm and beautiful, and with one accord we gathered in a circle on deck, for a reunion and an evening of song. By this time we had formed strong suspicions that

Mr. Morrison was a vocalist as well as a manipulator of the banjo, and Miss N. was delegated to inform him that his fellow-travelers believed that it was his duty to sing to us as a token of gratitude for the recovery of his voice. He acknowledged the force of the argument and gave us a fine sentimental song in good style, but we were in a jolly mood and clam.red for something of a more lively and vivacious character, and then this was the song he sang, with banjo accompaniament:

The Irish Christening at Tipperary.

"'Twas down in that place Tipperary,
  Where they're so airy and so contrary,
  They cut up the devil's figary,
    When they christened my beautiful boy.
  In the corner the piper sat winkin',
  And a blinkin', and a thinkin',
  And a naggin of punch he was drinkin',
    And wishing the parents great joy.
  When home from the church they came with
  Father Tom and big Micky Bannigan,
  Scores of as purty boys and girls
    As ever ye'd ax to see, when in flew the door
  And Hogan the tinker, and Lathering Lannigan
  Kicked up a row and wanted to know
  Why they weren't axed to the spree.

    And the baby set up such a squalling,
    And such a bawling and caterwauling,
    And the nurse on the mother was calling,
      There was a time "mon um ga joy"!
    The piper his chanter was droning,
    And a groaning, and a moaning,
    The ould woman set up the croaning
      When they christened sweet Danny the boy.

"Th' aristocracy came to the party,
  There was McCarty, light and hearty,
  Wid Florence Bedalia Fogarty,
    (She says that's the French for her name),
  Dionasius Alphonso Mulroony,
  Oh, so loony and so spoony,
  Wid the charmin' Evangeline Mooney,
    Of society she was the crame.

Cora Terasa Maud McCann,
Algernon Rouke and Lulu McCafferty,
Reginald Marmaduke Maurice Megan,
 Clarence Ignatius McGuirk,
Cornelius Horatio Flaherty's son,
Adelaide Grace and Doctor O'Rafferty,
Eva McLoughlin, Cora Muldoon,
 And Brigadier General Burke.

> They were dancing the Polka Mazurka,
> 'Twas a worker, ne'er a shirker,
> The Varsoviana La Turker
> And the Polka row-dow was divine.
> They marched and then went into luncheon,
> Oh, such punchin' and such scrunchin',
> They were busy as bees at the munchin'
> Wid coffee, tea, whisky and wine.

"There was all sorts of tay—there was Schow-chong.
And there was Ning-yong, and there was Ding-dong,
Wid Oolong, and Toolong, and Boolong,
 And tay that was made in Japan.
There was sweetmeats imported from Java,
And from Guava, and from Havre,
In the four-masted ship the Minarva,
 That came from beyant Hindoostan.
Cowld ice creams and cream that was hot,
Roman punch froze up in snowballs and sparagrass.
"Patte de foi gras," whatever that manes,
 Made out of goose livers and grease;
Red-headed ducks wid salmon and peas,
Bandy-legged frogs and Peruvian ostriches,
Bottle-nosed pickerel, woodcock and snipe,
 And everything else that would plaze.

> After dinner of course we had spaking,
> There was handshaking, there was leave-taking,
> In the corner ould mothers match-making,
> Wid other such innocent sins.
> And we drank a good health to each other,
> Then to each brother, then to each mother,
> But the last toast I thought I would smother,
> When they hoped that the next would be twins!"

His inimitable manner and excellent vocalism gave great delight, and for an encore he gave us another song, equally new and equally amusing.

Then we began the "old" songs, and our college friends, Mr. A. and young Mr. L., gave us the "Romance of the Cape," which Mr. Morrison also knew, and accompanied with the banjo:

"There came to the Cape a lady in crape,
 Of whom you may not hear;
They wrote her name in the visitors' book
 As a lady from Gardinier.
And with her was seen a lady in green,
 Of whom you may hear more;
Her husband was drown'd off Long Island Sound,
 So sea-green weeds she wore.

"And when with a clang the dinner-bell rang,
 To the banquet hall they sped,
They sat remote at the table-d'hôte,
 While the boarders sat at the head.
Oh, the boarders laughed as their wine they quaffed,
 Loud laughed each little child;
As they ate their chowder they laughed the louder,
 But these neither ate nor smiled.

"And when 'neath the pines they baited their lines
 And fished in mute despair,
The fisherman asked, as he shot through the blast,
 'Won't you give us a lock of your hair?'
'My husband is dead,' the green lady said,
 'A drownéd man is he;
I would he would rise, with his pale blue eyes
 And speak one word to me.'

"These words that she uttered were scarcely muttered,
 When her line grew heavy as lead,
And up rose a creature whose every feature,
 Resembled her husband dead!
'Come hither,' said he, 'to the deep blue sea;'
 And he tugged so hard at her line,
That he pulled her down, in her sea-green gown,
 While she sang 'Forever Thine!'"

"Then go, if you can, to the classic Cape Ann
   And stop at Hotel de Clare,
And view, without fainting, a beautiful painting
   That hangs in the parlor there.
This painting was made by the artist O'Quade,
   And on it two faces are seen—
The man who was drowned off Long Island Sound,
   And his wife, the lady in green."

Mr. Howe, our handsome young purser, was here persuaded to sing "The Light-house by the Sea" (that some of us had heard him humming to himself), and we all joined in the chorus.

THE LIGHT-HOUSE BY THE SEA.

"There's a light! there's a light,
   And it shines far out at sea—
'Tis a beacon so bright
   From my true-love to me.
There's a light! there's a light!
   In a light-house by the sea.

"In a light-house by the sea,
   There's a sweet face waits for me;
     Whene'er I'm away
     She waits day by day
For the white sails far over the foam;
   When storms rage high at night,
   Her lamps are always bright;
   She's the pride of my heart,
So steer, my lads, for home.

"Many a day since last I saw her face,
   And gazed in her eyes,
   Their loving truth to trace.
   We'll meet ne'er to part,
   For with her I'll remain.
   I am coming, yes, I'm coming
   To you, sweet lass, again.

"When storms rage high at sea,
   Ye ho, my lads, ye ho!
She waits for me,
   Ye ho, my lads, ye ho!

In a light-house by the sea,
A sweet face waits for me.
Whene'er I'm away,
She waits day by day
For the white sails far over the foam.
When storms rage high at night,
Her lamps are always bright ;
She's the pride of my heart,
So steer, lads, steer for home."

After this one of our number gave a recitation as follows :

"I stood on the steps of the Hoffman
And gazed at the living tide,
Of vehicles down the middle,
And people up either side.
And I saw a maid in her beauty,
In a shawl of real cashmere,
Step down from out of a carriage,
While her robe got caught in the rear !

"Oh, the robe was of *moire antique*,
A very expensive rag ;
But a skirt peeped out beneath,
And that was a coffee bag !
I knew it once held coffee,
Though now 'twas another thing,
For on it was "Fine old Java,"
Y, marked with store blacking !

"And as she gained the sidewalk,
And the muslin again was furled,
I thought how those outskirts and inskirts,
Were like men's hearts in the world !
How many a Pharisee humbug,
Plays a life-long game of brag,
His words all silk and velvet,
And his heart but a coffee bag !

"And I turned me into the Hoffman,
For my heart was beginning to sink,
And I told the tale to a comrade,
And it "rung him in" for a drink !
And as we imbibed the cocktails,
I then and there confessed,
When I thought how I liked the poison,
That I was as bad as the rest !"

Then Miss N., being pressed to sing, gave us that beautiful serenade by Samuel Lover, found in "Handy Andy":

> It is the chime the hour draws near,
>   When you and I must sever,
> Alas, it may be many a year,
>   And it may be forever!
>
> You said my heart was cold and stern,
>   You doubted love when strongest,
> In future years you'll live to learn,
>   Proud hearts can love the longest.
>
> Oh, sometimes think when press'd to hear,
>   When flippant tongues beset thee,
> That all must love thee when thou'rt near,
>   But I can ne'er forget thee,
>
> The changeful sand doth only know,
>   The shallow tide and latest;
> The rocks have mark'd its highest flow,
>   The deepest and the greatest.
>
> And deeper still the flood-marks grow,
>   So since the hour I met thee,
> The more the tide of time doth flow,
>   The less can I forget thee!

This tender love-song brought upon us a more quiet mood and we lapsed from gay to grave, and parted for the night with the sentiment of sweet hymns—hallowed by fond recollections of home and sanctuary—on our lips and in our hearts. One by one my fellow-travelers retired to their state-rooms, while I, in a reflective mood, still kept my seat on the deck and gazed on the moon, the stars and on the silvery sea. I was reminded of those lines of Tom Moore:

> See how beneath the moonbeam's smile
>   Yon little billow heaves its breast;
> It foams and sparkles for a while,
>   And, murmuring, then subsides to rest.
>
> So man, the sport of bliss and care,
>   Rises on Time's eventful sea,
> And, having swell'd a moment there,
>   Thus melts into eternity.

CHAPTER VIII.

The Spanish Main.

> Hark, do you hear the sea? The murmuring surge,
> That on the unnumber'd idle pebbles chafes?
> —*King Lear.*

"THE Spanish Main" is, technically speaking, the *main-land*, or coast, of that part of South America skirting the Caribbean Sea from Honduras on the west, to the Gulf of Paria on the east, a distance, following the coast line, of about two thousand miles. It is said by lexicographers that this coast received the name of "The Spanish Main" from early English voyagers to the West Indies and colonists in those islands, they referring to it as the *main-land* discovered and possessed by the Spaniards long before. That this is the origin of the name, or that it *only* refers to the *land* or *coast*, is a mooted point, as many historians speak of "The Spanish Main" as that part of the *Caribbean Sea*, or indeed the whole of it, that washes the shores of what is now known as Central America, United States of Colombia, and Venezuela, and which was first sailed by Columbus, Americus Vespucius and other Spanish navigators and explorers. In this view it receives its name of "The Spanish Main," in the signification that the *main* is the ocean or sea. Many historical accounts, and romances without number, have been written about the pirates and buccaneers of "The Spanish Main," and these were the wild sea-rovers of the Caribbean Sea that plundered and burnt the rich Spanish galleons as they sailed from their South American possessions loaded with precious metals to enrich the sovereigns and grandees of Spain.

While there is a decided distinction in the original signification or meaning of the terms "buccaneers" and "pirates," there was but little difference in the manner in which these gentlemen of the quarter-deck conducted themselves while pursuing their adopted profession.

We hear of a noted pirate named Morgan, who was a Welshman, and had his headquarters on the island of Jamaica. He flourished about the middle of the seventeenth century, and became such a terror to the merchant marine of England, and became so rich withal, that Charles Second, the "Merry Monarch" of England, knighted him and made him Lieutenant-Governor of the Island of Jamaica, where he lived to a good old age, and died full of honor, and, of course, in the consolations of religion. Some of his deeds, when he first became a freebooter, were so desperate as to seem the frenzy of a madman. Once with a small boat, manned only by thirty men, he captured the ship of the vice-admiral of the Spanish fleet! In the darkness of the night they rowed with muffled oars to the side of the great ship. While doing so, Morgan himself was busy boring holes in the bottom of his boat, so that when the battle commenced his men would fight with greater desperation, knowing that the only means of escape or saving their own lives would be in defeating the Spaniards and possessing themselves of the ship.

Cutlass in hand they climbed up the sides of the vessel, cut down the sentries before an alarm could be given, and, before the vice-admiral knew that an enemy was on board, Morgan was in his cabin holding a pistol to his head and demanding unconditional surrender! But Morgan finally commanded a fleet of fifteen small vessels, and a force of men numbering over one thousand, and with these he took cities on the mainland, and loaded his ships with the gold, and silver, and merchandise of which he plundered them.

Sometimes, when he had taken possession of a city, he demanded a sum as ransom that was so enormous that the citizens said that it could not be raised, but after a few of them were tortured most horribly, the ransom money was invariably produced.

But to my mind the most interesting history connected with these beautiful seas, are the annals of the French buccaneers. They were originally a simple company of French settlers who established themselves on some of the smaller islands of the West Indies shortly after their discovery by the Spaniards, and supported themselves comfortably in the primitive occupation of hunting wild cattle, horses, buffalo and deer. After a time they turned their attention to commerce, and began to tan the hides of these animals for exportation, and which they sold to the Dutch trading vessels. They also cured the flesh and sold it to mariners and others. The original inhabitants of these islands were the Caribee Indians, and they, being cannibals, were accustomed to cut their prisoners of war in pieces and cure their flesh upon a species of hurdle or wooden grate, called *barbacoa*, and then smoking them under open sheds called *boucans*. So, as these French settlers treated their beef and venison as the Caribees did their prisoners, they were called *boucaniers* or buccaneers. But soon the greedy Spaniards, jealous of their happiness and prosperity, began to persecute them and finally drove them away from their homes in these smaller islands. They took refuge in the island of San Domingo, then called Hispaniola, and for a long time pursued their vocation as herdsmen and hunters in the immense unexplored interior of this great island, without their existence there being known to the Spaniards, who had settlements on the eastern side of the island, and who claimed the whole of San Domingo.

It was not until they had become very numerous, and had pushed their hunting-grounds up to their plantations and settlements, that the Spanish colonists learnt the existence and felt the power of the buccaneers. Then the Spaniards called to their aid troops from Spain and Cuba to expel the intruders from the island. For twenty years the struggle between the buccaneers and the Spanish troops was continued, and all the cunning and inhuman cruelty for which the Spanish nation is noted was brought to bear on these French *boucaniers* who, up to this time, were simple herdsmen and hunters. The Spaniards poisoned and otherwise destroyed their game, hoping thus to starve them out of the island.

Shakespeare makes Shylock say to his Christian enemies, "The villainy you teach me, I will execute, and it shall go hard but I will *better* the instruction."

So it was with these buccaneers; driven to desperation by the persecutions and cruelties of the Spaniards, they united with certain English rovers, or *fillibusters*, as they were called by the Spaniards, and commenced a series of depredations on the vessels sailing under the Spanish flag, and were so successful that they soon became greatly feared. The villainy taught them by the Spanish they began to execute, and in their ferocity and cold-blooded cruelties they "bettered the instruction."

This was in the latter part of the 17th century, when Charles II. was on the throne of Spain, Louis XIV. on the throne of France, and William III. on the throne of England. Each of these nations had great interests in these West India Islands. The buccaneers were led by brave and fearless men, and their success was so great against the Spaniards, and in maintaining their foothold on the island of San Domingo, that France hastened to recognize them, and appointed a governor to represent France in the ownership of one-half of the island. And the king of France was not too honest to receive a tenth of the value of all the prizes taken by the buccaneers, which was regularly paid by them to the governor of their part of the island. As this is history, it can also be stated, without fear of contradiction, that the governor appointed by Louis XIV. over French San Domingo was a famous buccaneer named "Ducasse"! One of the strongholds of the buccaneers was the island of Tortuga, situated on the north side of the island of Hayti (or Santo Domingo, as it was then called), about seven miles off from the main island. This island of Tortuga was forty miles in circumference, and was surrounded, except on the southern side, by a chain of rocks called "Coles de Fer," and which made it, practically, unapproachable, except on the side next the island of Hayti, which is called Tortuga Channel. "Tortuga" merely means "tortoise," or "turtle," and there are several other islands in these tropical seas by the same name. The one above alluded to is the one that the English recently threatened to take from Hayti unless certain old claims were settled. Here, in this almost impregnable island fortress, the buccaneers lived for many years, and were never conquered. Peace was finally made with them by recognizing their rights and appointing their chieftains to lucrative and honorable positions under the Spanish, French and English governments in these West India Islands. Many of their descendants still live on the islands and are far from feeling ashamed of their noted ancestors. Among the names of these noted chiefs, whose fearless and bloody deeds made them the terror of the seas, we find those of Montbars, Laurent, and John Hepburn: the first a Scotchman of good family; the second a Frenchman of royal birth—said to have been the son of the Man with the Iron Mask and nephew to Louis XIV.— and the third an Englishman who bought a large tract of land in Santo Domingo, but who made his land operations secondary to his more profitable ventures on the sea in plundering Spanish galleons.

The romances of the Spanish Main also tell of a certain "Nativa del Roco," a beautiful girl, granddaughter of Hepburn, the Englishman, born on the island of Tortuga, and almost worshiped by the buccaneers as their good angel, and who often accompanied them in their desperate encounters, and who seemed to have borne a charmed life—a sort of a Mascot on shipboard, as it were. But this may have been only a creation of the romancer's brain, and it is hardly worth while to speculate upon or investigate the truth or falsity of the story. There is enough in the veritable history of these buccaneers of the Spanish Main to fully satisfy the cravings of all lovers of the horrible, or to arouse in the minds of all humanitarians a sense of gratitude that a better era has dawned upon the world, and that no longer do men commit these dreadful and wholesale murders on the ocean—that we may sail upon these beautiful seas having no dangers to contend with but those of the elements, thanking God that the days of pirates and buccaneers have passed away forever!

GUZMAN BLANCO, PRESIDENT OF VENEZUELA.

CHAPTER IX.

Venezuela.

AT daylight I was aroused by Mr. Wilkinson, who informed me that the mountains of Venezuela were in sight. There they were in their majesty, rising four to five thousand feet right out of the Caribbean Sea! Venezuela is pronounced in the Spanish in four syllables instead of five, viz., "Ven-ez-wee-la," with the accent on the third syllable. Some of the islands on the eastern coast were discovered by Columbus in 1498, and the whole coast was explored the following year by Francis de Ojeda and Americus Vespucci. The name Venezuela means "Little Venice," and was given to it by these two last-named Spanish navigators, who found in Lake Maracaibo a number of Indian villages, built on piles on the borders of the lake, which so reminded them of Venice that they named that portion of the country Venezuela, or Little Venice, and subsequently the whole country was called Venezuela. It comprises an area of 439,120 square miles, being about as large as our two largest states, Texas and California, combined. It has, at present, a total population of a little over two millions of inhabitants. It is very mountainous, and some parts of it are yet unexplored, but are known to be inhabited by barbarous races of Indians. Some of the mountain peaks reach an altitude of 15,000 feet, but they generally range from 3,000 to 9,000 feet in height. Back of the coast ranges, and along the great river Orinoco, are immense grassy plains, or prairies, where vast herds of horned cattle, horses and mules roam in a wild state, and are hunted for their hides and hair, which articles form quite an important item in the list of exports of Venezuela.

The climate varies with the elevation. In the low regions, not rising above 2,000 feet from the sea, it is very hot. At an elevation of from 2,000 to 7,000 feet, the climate is delightful and healthy. But where the country rises above 7,000 feet, it generally becomes uninhabitable because of the perpetual mists which hang over these regions, and the terrible hail and snow-storms which visit them.

Like other tropical countries, it has but two seasons, the wet and the dry. The dry season is called summer, and usually extends from about the middle of November to the middle of April, while the rainy season, or winter, fills up the balance of the year. It is a very fertile country, and is certainly well watered, for, besides the great river Orinoco, with its course of 1,500 miles, and 400 navigable tributary streams, there are 230 rivers that flow into the Caribbean Sea and the gulfs of Venezuela and Paria, and several hundred other lesser streams flowing into Maracaibo and other lakes.

Some of the products of Venezuela, in its vegetable kingdom, are, coffee, cocoa, cotton, indigo, tobacco, cacao (or chocolate), sugar-cane, plantains, maize, wheat, and a great variety of tropical fruits. Only an exceedingly small portion of the whole area of Venezuela is cultivated, yet the export trade in the products mentioned, especially coffee and cacao, is quite large and rapidly increasing. It is estimated that 350,000 acres are devoted to the cultivation of the coffee shrub, and 55,000 acres to the cacao, or chocolate tree.

The exceeding fertility of the soil will always be one of the great and lasting sources of wealth in the country. The mineral wealth of Venezuela is also very great, but its immense primeval forests, opulent with their varieties of rare and valu-

SCENE IN VENEZUELA.—THE FERN-PALM.

able woods, are more interesting to the traveler than the mines or the plantations. Here are found mahogany, satin-wood, ebony, rosewood, *caoutchouc*, or India-rubber tree, as well as many very valuable dye-woods, gum-trees, and medicinal plants. Here, also, is the celebrated *cinchona*-tree, the bark of which is so well known under the name of Peruvian bark. This valuable medicinal bark was used by the Peruvian Indians centuries ago, and was introduced to medical science throughout the world through the agency of the Countess Cinchon, in the 17th century. She was the wife of the Viceroy of Peru, and having, by its use, been cured of an intermittent fever, on her return to Spain she gave its virtues wide notoriety, and assisted largely in extending the knowledge of the curative properties of this wonderful product of South America. Since that time the tree has been known as the "Cinchona," and its native name has been lost sight of.

The region below the level of 3,000 feet is the country of the palms — the sago palm, the *chiquichique*, and the *yagua*, whose fibrous tufts are converted into cordage, while the *yagua* also yields an excellent oil. Then there are the giant royal palm, the wax palm, the fan palm and the cocoanut palm, from which cocoanut oil is manufactured, and several other varieties of palms. But these great forests are rich, also, in the animal kingdom. Any number of circuses could be well stocked with "rare and wonderful animals," from the forest of Venezuela, "each one of which alone would be worth the price of admission." The jaguar, panther, tiger, tapir, black bear, peccary, badger, and fifteen varieties of monkeys constantly on hand. Also, a very fine line of sloths, armadillos, and several varieties of ant-eaters, while in serpents, a varied assortment of boa-constrictors, varying in length from fifteen to fifty feet (to suit customers), the cayman, the iguana, the basilisk and chameleon can always be found in the forests of the mountains or the swamps of the lowlands. The *truga venados*, or deer swallower, is an interesting reptile for a pet, while fifteen other varieties of large snakes — most of which are venomous — immense spiders, bats and centipedes, help to form this happy family inhabiting the wilds of Venezuela.

A few words relating to the history of Venezuela and its present government can scarcely be avoided in giving an account of a visit to its capital and some of its sea-ports. And yet, how difficult it is to epitomize a history so remarkable and varied as hers. As I reflect upon the struggles of these South American nations to free themselves from the Spanish yoke, after having visited the scenes of many of their battles with their relentless enemies, and having seen the beautiful and costly monuments erected to the memory of their patriotic dead, I am filled with admiration for their patriotism and valor, and accord to them much of the same noble spirit that animated our own forefathers in their long struggle to free themselves from a foreign yoke. The name of Bolivar, the liberator of Venezuela, is honored and venerated there as our own Washington is here.

The "United States of Venezuela" is now a republic, and has been for the last fifteen to eighteen years, governed wisely by Guzman Blanco, who is still the president. July 5, 1811, was the time that Venezuela proclaimed its independence, and the day is still celebrated with great enthusiasm every year, much in the same manner as we celebrate the 4th of July, the birthday of our own nationality. But Spain did not give up this rich country without a protracted struggle, lasting until 1823, when she reluctantly relinquished it.

But to return to my ship, which is now rapidly approaching the harbor of Puerto Cabello. We had to lay-to off the harbor waiting till sunrise, so that in accordance with the regulations of all fortified harbors in Spanish countries we could then

SCENE IN VENEZUELA.—THE COCOA-PALM.

enter. I sat and watched the sun rise from out of the sea. What a glorious sight! The mountains have a purple hue. Some of the taller peaks were above the clouds.

> "Night's candles are burnt out, and jocund day
> Stands tiptoe on the misty mountain-tops."

Puerto Cabello lies in a half-moon or half-circle of the mountains. It is an excellent harbor, defended from storms by a long sandspit, and defended (by courtesy only) from enemies by a venerable fort, valuable now only in memory of its past history, or as it serves as a prison for a score or two of miserable offenders against the law or policy of the State. Puerto Cabello has a population of 10,000. It is nestled under the shadow of the great mountains and has the long narrow streets peculiar to all Spanish cities. The inhabitants are of all colors and all speak the Spanish language only. The climate is hot, and, at certain seasons, quite unhealthy. Being one of the best harbors on the coast, it is a place of considerable importance. The imports here amount to about five millions of dollars a year, while the exports are nearly double that sum. In company with Mr. Livingston and his son I took a carriage drive four or five miles back into the country to a pretty place called San Esteban, which is the country residence of six or eight German families who keep stores in Puerto Cabello. Our driver was black, and as he spoke no English, and as we haggled over but a few words of Spanish, the continuity of vocal communication from the inside to the outside seat was frequently broken, and soon, by mutual consent, born of necessity, was abandoned altogether. But our colored brother, though speechless, was politely mindful of our being "strangers within his gates," and frequently stopped to point out a fine mountain view, or to cull a tropical flower or plant, which he presented to us with an easy grace, as if to say, "Speech is silver, silence is golden, and I can only speak to you in the language of flowers." But he didn't forget to exact four dollars for the two hours' ride, all the same!

Along the road-side we saw occasionally a small pile of stones and a rude wooden cross stuck up beside it. These marked the graves of some poor fellows who had met violent deaths and were buried where they were killed. A Venezuelan on our steamer, who imbibed a good deal from divers bottles which he had in his state-room, told us how that he was traveling on horseback with a friend one day in Venezuela, and that they had but one bottle of brandy between them. Now, if his friend had the same amiable weakness for drinking as the narrator of the story had, this one bottle of brandy must have assumed the same discouraging outlook to them as did the cruse of oil to the widow when another individual proposed to share it with her. However, as the distance they had to travel was over ten miles, they agreed that they would only take a drink when they came to one of these wayside crosses. For a time all went well, the crosses were frequent, and so were the drinks; but after a time they seemed to have struck a very peaceful piece of road—not a cross was to be seen! Things were getting serious, till suddenly one of these "two souls with but a single thought," leaped from his horse, spread out his arms in the shape of a cross and said, in effect, and in Spanish, "Eureka! Let's take a drink!" How can I doubt the story when I have seen the crosses?

Returning to the harbor we found that two small vessels had just come from "Los Roccas," a number of dangerous reefs and sand-islands about seventy-five miles north of the main-land, and were loaded with "booby" eggs and turtles. The "booby" is a bird similar to the sea-gull, and its eggs are gathered at Los Roccas in great quantities, and sold at the sea-port towns for food. One of the vessels had twenty thousand, and the other twelve thousand of these eggs. The

SCENE IN VENEZUELA.—FRUIT MERCHANT ON A COUNTRY ROAD WAITING FOR CUSTOMERS.

native colored women had already bought many, and had boiled them hard and were carrying around on their heads trays full of them to sell. I bought one, and in regular picnic style, picked off the shell, and, having seasoned it with a pinch of salt and pepper mixed, bit into it rather gingerly at first, but finding it of excellent flavor, I finished it and another one with a good deal of gusto. These eggs are just the size of our common hen's eggs, and sell for eighty cents per hundred.

The forty-one turtles which formed part of the cargo of these little vessels, were transferred to our steamer, and we carried them to New York. They varied in weight from fifty to two hundred pounds each, and as they lay helplessly on their backs on the main deck of our vessel, they were kept alive by being thoroughly drenched with sea-water every few hours during the passage to New York.

Our steamer was being unloaded of a portion of her cargo of general merchandise by a large gang of half-naked negroes, and the little mules were drawing it away from the dock in big-wheeled carts. Each of these little animals has to draw nine barrels of flour at a load, which seems almost impossible when you reflect that he is himself almost small enough to be thrust into an empty barrel. Water is also carried on the backs of these wonderfully strong, tireless and sure-footed beasts. Two full-sized barrels, full of water, are hung over his back—one on each side—and with them he will walk along, the patient slave of his master or driver. It is a queer sight to see a line of these " burros," as they are called, coming in from the country Indian file, loaded with bags of coffee. There are but one hundred and fourteen miles of railroad in all Venezuela, and the carrying of the greater portion of all the products of the country to the cities and to the sea-ports, is done by these sturdy little animals. In the eternal fitness of things, mules were certainly created expressly for use in mountainous countries.

While our steamer was being unloaded of merchandise, and again loaded, partly with coffee, hides, cocoa, etc., we had abundant time to stroll around the town and see the many sights curious to Northern eyes. The plaza is quite a pretentious one, and though not well-shaded, seems to be well-cared for, and, with its plants and flowers, presented a pleasing appearance. There are public baths by the sea-shore inclosed with strong palings, like a poultry yard, as a protection from sharks. But the "Banos del Mar" of Puerto Cabello, like those I saw in Havana, seem to be neglected and but little used. Cleanliness is far from being one of the cardinal virtues of the inhabitants of these hot countries. The vultures seem to be the chief scavengers in and about the town, and in virtue of their office are exempt from serving as targets to sportsmen. The public market was well worth a visit. Here we saw all kinds of vegetables indigenous to the soil, a great variety of parrots, and troopials, and other bright-hued birds. We were importuned to buy monkeys, which our good angels protected us from doing. The tiger-skins were more seductive and less noisy, while the celebrated "casava" bread was the most attractive of all. It is made of the root called *yuca mandioca*, which, when grated, is put into a bag and the juice, which is poisonous, is pressed out; after which the grated root is rolled out into thin round slices twenty-eight inches in diameter and about an eighth of an inch thick. After being dried in the sun it is ready to be eaten. I ate some of it and found it quite palatable. But I don't hanker after it.

The market-house is quite large, being, I should judge, 150 feet long by 50 or 60 feet wide. It was filled with a chattering crowd of people of all colors, and all speaking Spanish. They seemed good-natured and even jolly, and the women really seemed quite inclined to flirt, which filled me with alarm, and I urged upon my less timid companions the importance of hurrying back to our ark of safety, the steamer "Philadelphia."

CHAPTER X.

Canal Victims!—La Guayra.

AS we lay at the dock at Puerto Cabello, taking in our cargo of coffee, the French mail steamer "Ville de Marseilles," came in and dropped her anchor within one hundred feet and right abreast of us. She plies between Havre and Colon, touching at several of the West India Islands, and also at La Guayra and Porto Cabello on the Venezuelan coast. She is a large steamer, being three hundred and two feet long and thirty-seven feet beam. Her carrying capacity is two thousand tons, and she has accommodations for eighty-four cabin passengers and one hundred and fifty second cabin and steerage. She had a large number of Frenchmen, and fifty or more "Jamaica niggers" all going to Colon as laborers on De Lessep's canal. Poor fellows, I pitied them, for I could look upon them in no other light than as "lambs led to the slaughter." Ignorant of the deadly influences of the climate, and deluded by promises of high wages, they go in droves to labor on the great ship canal across the Isthmus of Panama. They go, but few, if any, ever return! Exposure to the deadly miasma of the night and terrible heat of the day, with insufficient food and impure water, too ignorant to use precaution or to practice any healing methods, the fever makes them its easy victims, and they die off like sheep with the murrain, and are buried like dogs. A few of the more intelligent and cleanly of the laborers, especially Americans, survive to escape, and the tales they tell of the daily horrors witnessed on that canal, would be almost too incredible for belief, if not amply corroborated by many others who have been witnesses of the same dreadful state of affairs. And so, as I look at these honest French peasants and at these fat and laughing " Jamaica niggers" on this great French steamer, I repeat, " Poor fellows, they are like lambs led to the slaughter, they will lay their bones on the banks of the De Lessep's canal, and meet their death 'unwept, unhonored and unsung'!"

Leaving Puerto Cabello at nightfall, we steamed away for La Guayra, about seventy or eighty miles easterly, which place we reached the next morning. La Guayra is the sea-port of the City of Caracas, the capital of Venezuela, which lies seven miles back from the sea, and over the coast range of mountains, on a lovely plain called the Valley of Caracas. La Guayra, unlike Puerto Cabello, has no harbor at all, and is entirely exposed to all northerly winds. The coast line is at almost all seasons of the year crested with foam from the breakers which go tumbling and roaring upon it. But there is good anchorage here, and vessels lie in safety except in times of storm, when they have to slip their cables and put to sea. As we came to anchor within about a half a mile from shore, the mountains towered above us to the height of nine thousand feet, and seemingly at an angle of forty-five degrees from the deck of our steamer. The mountains here are very steep and gloomy looking. There are on the face of them occasional patches of green that look as if they might be in a state of cultivation, but, for the most part they seem to be densely wooded. The city, which has but about ten thousand inhabitants, is irregularly built, partly in the valley by the side of the Caribbean Sea, and partly up the foot-hills of the mountain. The streets are exceedingly narrow, and where they lead up the foot-hills are very steep. There are but few good residences here, nine-tenths of the population seeming to be, like the children of Gibbeon—hewers of wood and drawers of water—and live in adobe huts or thatched cottages, with but very few of what we would call the common necessaries of life.

Along the shore, extending the entire length of this straggling city, is a strong sea-wall, built to protect it from the long heavy swells sent in by the trade-winds. On an elevation to the right of the city, and overlooking the entire town and harbor—if the anchorage can be so called—is an ancient-looking fort built by the Spaniards in the old colonial days, as a protection against the buccaneers. A small garrison is kept there, and a slight show of the " pride, pomp and circumstance of glorious war " is still kept up, but it is simply ludicrous, and reminds one of the old soldier in Goldsmith's " Deserted Village," who " shouldered his crutch and showed how fields were won."

On an eminence to the left is another fort, a relic of the past, and still further up the mountain-side there is yet another really picturesque ruin of an old fort, which dates back to the sixteenth century. I am glad to say, however, that Guzman Blanco, the President of Venezuela, is taking care of these old forts, protecting them from further decay, and repairing some of the ravages that time has made. Whether he does this in a utilitarian sense, or merely to preserve the antique beauty of their architecture, and as memorials of those early days of Venezuelan history, I do not know. To the traveler whose mind dwells more on the "strange and eventful history" of these Spanish-speaking countries than on the present state of their affairs, the old Spanish fortresses, with their queer little Moorish watch-towers, have a fascination and attraction decidedly greater than any of their more recent structures.

But to return to the so-called harbor of La Guayra—though all vessels have to be loaded and unloaded by lighters, there is more business done here than at all the other sea-ports of

Venezuela combined. These lighters are built like whale-boats, only much heavier and larger. They are made of lignum-vitæ and iron-wood, and cost twelve hundred dollars each. They are handled very skillfully by natives, and carry great loads back and forth from the vessels with perfect safety, landing them through the surf without wetting any of the goods. A smaller size of boats convey passengers to and from the shore. Sometimes the passengers have to be carried from the boats (after touching the beach), through the foam of the surf to the dry land, on the backs of the boatmen. But this was not the case while we were there, as the sea was comparatively smooth.

The morning we reached La Guayra there were anchored there two Venezuelan gun-boats, two English war steamers, and two English gun-boats, three barks, one full-rigged ship, three large schooners, and fourteen small coasting vessels from ten to seventy-five tons each. Before going to Caracas a Spanish war-steamer, an English mail-steamer, a Dutch mail-steamer and three large sailing vessels came to anchor near our steamer.

The City of Caracas is but seven miles from La Guayra, "as the crow flies," but the nearest wagon-road to it is over twenty-four miles long. There is another route more nearly direct over the mountain, which, however, can only be traveled by mules and donkeys, and it was by this path in the old times that communication was had between the two cities. The wagon-road is of a much later date, having been constructed when the growing importance and wealth of Caracas rendered it necessary for the easier transportation of heavy and bulky freights.

But now the locomotive creeps up and around these solemn mountains, and darts across the yawning chasms in a sinuous trail, waking the echoes with its shrill scream, and disturbing the slumbers or pleasures of the lions, and tigers, and boa-constrictors, of which these mountains are full. The Caracas and La Guayra Railroad is twenty-four miles long, and has fourteen bridges, eight tunnels and a fabulous number of curves. Indeed, it is said that one of the engineers who surveyed the line died of grief, because he could not put in one more curve. The road is narrow gauge and was built and is owned by an English company. The fare either way (first class), is two dollars and fifty cents! The freight rate on a bag of coffee (130 lbs.), from Caracas to La Guayra, is one dollar! What is the Standard Oil Company or any other Yankee monopoly in comparison to that? But the Englishmen don't get it all by any manner of means. The "concession" which has to be obtained from the government before a railroad or similar work can be commenced, always costs a very pretty penny in the first place, and a continual "divy" of profits forever afterwards. And this leads me to say that whatever of indolence may be charged to the Spanish character in these tropical countries, it draws the line at the collection of customs and taxes. In those departments of labor, nothing can exceed the industry of the government officials, except it may be the ingenuity which those individuals display in getting a share of it into their own pockets. Though no passports are required, yet you have to pay a custom-house fee when you enter and when you depart from the country.

I had the pleasure of meeting at La Guayra, Mr. Winfield S. Bird, the American consul at that port. Mr. Bird has resided here for several years, is a fluent speaker of the Spanish tongue, and has become very familiar with all the characteristics of the natives of this interesting portion of America, as also with the resources of Venezuela and her adjoining republics. My acquaintance with him was of but two or three days' duration, during which time, however, he showed me every attention and contributed much to the pleasure of my stay there. At parting he handed me a document which he had written for me, which upon opening, I found to be two poems upon La Guayra. "No. 1 was written," he said, "for this latitude, and as he was partial to La Guayra, it expressed his sentiments, while No. 2 indicates pretty clearly the impressions and feelings of transient Americans who stay here only long enough to see the dark side of the picture." Only those that have visited these old Spanish cities can fully appreciate the humor of No. 2, and I did not stay at La Guayra long enough to become very much saturated with the enthusiasm which permeates No. 1.

I. La Guayra.

Oh, tranquil *paraiso*, nestled near the placid sea,
La Guayra, *mi querida*, I must bid adieu to thee!
My boat is tossing in the surf, the twilight settles down,
Asi pues, mi despedida—adios, my dear old town.

Oh, gorgeous, cloud-kissed mountains, that majestically rise
Far up into the azure of the lovely tropic skies,
Frown never, but forever with the smile of pity greet
The home of *mis recuerdos* sweetly sleeping at your feet.

Thou restless and resistless *olas* that, with ceaseless roar
And sheets of white *espuma*, dash upon the rocky shore,
Beat lightly and break brightly, with thy changeless melody,
On the beautiful *orillas* of this haven by the sea.

And thou, too, gentle mother earth, in moments of unrest,
Trembling with hollow thunders that re-echo in thy breast,
In pity spare La Guayra a recurrence of her woes—
The death and desolation of the *terremota* throes.

With fondest recollections and with heart sincere and true,
Guairëños queridisimos, receive my last adieu!
May God, *con mano mua*, ever graciously extend
To you the favor you have shown to your departing friend.

II. LA GUAYRA.

Adios to thee, La Guayra! city of the dark-eyed *gente*,
Land of *mucho calor* and of *dolce far niente*,
Home of the wailing donkey and the all-abounding flea,
Mañana, gracios á Dios! I bid adieu to thee.

Farewell, ye gloomy *casas, mejor dicho* prison cells,
Ye narrow, crooked *calles*, reeking with assorted smells,
Ye dirty little coffee shops and filthy *pulperias*,
Stinking stables, dingy *patios* and fetid *cañerias*.

Where beggars ride on horseback like Spanish cavaliers,
And vagabonds perambulate like jolly gamboliers,
Where the *lavanderas* wash your *ropa* when they feel inclined,
And hotel waiters strut around with shirt-tails out behind.

Good-by, ye Latin greasers! *su atento servidor*,
Que vaya bien, pues adios! my boat is on the shore;
Oh, dirty people, dirty houses, despicable spot,
Departing, I salute you in your dirtiness and rot.

Steaming and streaming with boiling perspiration,
Seething and breathing with hurried respiration,
La Guayra, *adios siempre, tierra tan caliente*,
Infernal clime of vicious rum and vilest *aguardiente*.

Notwithstanding the heat, the want of cleanliness, the lack of proper sewerage, and the degrading habits of a large proportion of its population, La Guayra is said to be a healthy city. It has played a prominent part in the history of the Spanish Main during the seventeenth and eighteenth centuries, having been more than once sacked by the pirates and buccaneers. In 1812 an earthquake reduced it to ruins, with the exception of its large and very substantial custom-house, which remained uninjured, except a huge crack across its massive door-sill, which souvenir of the dreadful visitor I viewed with interest.

All kinds of tropical fruits are very abundant here and are perpetually growing and ripening, so that "fruit in season," would be an unnecessary item to enumerate on a hotel or restaurant bill of fare at La Guayra.

The railway, as I said, is twenty-four miles long, and this to reach a place just seven miles distant. In eighteen miles it reaches an altitude of a little over three thousand feet. At times we had magnificent views of the sea and of La Guayra at our very feet, but so far off that the great ships at anchor looked like little toy boats, and the hundreds of lighters could hardly be seen at all. Sometimes we went rushing along the edge of a gorge that made me feel qualmish to look down into, and although it took two hours to run that twenty-four miles, it seemed to me that we went at a devil-may-care rate, and I breathed much easier when we reached the lovely valley of Caracas, three thousand five hundred feet above the level of the sea, and had a view of the old Spanish city in the distance.

THE CAPITOL AT CARACAS, VENEZUELA.

CHAPTER XI.

CARACAS.

AT the railway station at Caracas there were to be seen the usual crowd of hack-drivers and porters soliciting (in vorciferous Spanish) the pleasure of transporting passengers and their baggage to the hotels. Ignoring these and following the lead of Signor Rudloff, I walked a few steps and took a queer little street car which soon conveyed us through narrow streets, a mile or more, to the Hotel Saint Amand, which is pleasantly located on quite a wide street fronting the capitol and its handsome grounds. As my friend turned into a gloomy hallway and commenced to climb some dirty stairs, I supposed that he was merely calling at some business office before going to the hotel. But following on, "to take it all in," I was surprised to find that this gloomy old barracks was the "Hotel Saint Amand," the best hotel in the City of Caracas.

To give a pen picture of the primitive customs that prevail in this old caravansary would tax my descriptive powers beyond their limits. The building was evidently originally erected for a dwelling, and its large apartments have been partitioned off into smaller ones, and the walls of separation are made of merely half-inch boards and papered! The courtyard or *patio*, which is the characteristic of all dwellings in Spanish countries, is there; but instead of being "a thing of beauty and a joy forever," is but a receptacle for all sorts of rubbish. The bed-rooms being all on the second floor and arranged around this open court, their unhappy occupants have the full benefit of a variety of odors which are anything but agreeable to sensitive nostrils. My German friend soon had apartments assigned to us by the somewhat ancient señorita who presided as clerk over this delectable retreat. After making our toilets, we were piloted to another house, through the grounds of the capitol, where we took our meals. This was the portion of the Saint Amand, with a few similar rooms, where the guests are fed, and in truth I must say that the food was good, well cooked, well served and in ample variety. In the morning, coffee or chocolate is served in your sleeping-room, or on the balcony overlooking the court-yard aforesaid, and breakfast cannot be had before eleven o'clock. The interval between early morning coffee and breakfast is the pleasantest part of the day to walk or ride about the city, except, perhaps, an hour or two late in the afternoon when the heat of the middle of the day has somewhat subsided.

The foulness of the court-yard and back-yards, the utter lack of sanitary measures in all the necessary appurtenances of a hotel, and the abundant evidence of ignorance of all that pertains to cleanliness and health, led me to expect a nightly seance with bed-bugs, but in this I was agreeably disappointed. Nothing but the wicked and subtle flea disputed my claim to balmy sleep, tired nature's sweet restorer. But with a calm and serene spirit I successfully overcame his intrusive attentions sufficiently to obtain the necessary amount of sleep to knit up the ravelled sleeve of care, and emerge from my boudoir with a smiling face and refreshed body every morning.

On the train from La Guayra I was introduced to the resident British minister at Caracas, Mr. St. John, pronounced, however, *Sin* John ("English, you know"), who was a fine-looking and very courteous gentleman.

The Republic of Venezuela has lately had a serious misunderstanding with England regarding some boundary lines

RAILWAY STATION AT THE FOOT OF THE MOUNTAIN IN THE SUBURBS OF THE CITY OF CARACAS.

near English Guiana, the tract of territory in dispute assuming recently great importance by the discovery of very rich gold mines upon it. England, as is averred, assumes to own it, occupies it, and, anchoring her armored ships of war in several of the Venezuelan ports, very coolly says to the little republic, "What are you going to do about it?" Under these circumstances, President Guzman Blanco has given the British minister his papers, and diplomatic relations between the two countries have been severed. Mr. St. John has taken up his quarters on one of Her Majesty's war ships at La Guayra awaiting orders from his government, and his trip to Caracas was but to attend to some personal affairs. What the outcome will be, it is difficult to premise. President Blanco has offered to have the dispute arbitrated by the United States Government, which proposition was declined by England.

Almost immediately upon our arrival at Caracas we encountered a gentleman by the name of H. R. Hamilton, whose brogue determined his nationality, although an American by adoption, and whose pressing invitation to "go and have something," was proof that his residence of a few years in Caracas had not made him forget the custom that so unhappily prevails among so many of our countrymen. A drug store seemed the fashionable place for high-toned drinking in Caracas (as it often is here in the United States), and thither we proceeded. On our way we met Major Charles L. Scott, U. S. A., minister to Venezuela, residing at Caracas.

Mr. Hamilton, who is a prominent man in Caracas, and evidently occupies some confidential position "near the throne," immediately introduced us to our fellow-countryman. An introduction in every-day life at home is a very common and unimportant matter, and in many instances is a custom "more honored in the breach than in the observance," but in a foreign land, among strangers whose language is not understood, an influential introduction to a fellow-countryman is a very different affair, and assumes at once the complexion of a boon—a blessing—a pleasure that can only be appreciated by a traveler in such circumstances. Mr. Hamilton's thoughtful and courteous introduction to Major Scott produced a result, during our few days stay in the City of Caracas, which was all that a tourist's heart could wish, and will ever be remembered by me with feelings of the liveliest gratitude.

Major Charles L. Scott is a Virginian by birth. He went to California in 1849, and afterwards represented that state in Congress during the thirty-fifth and thirty-sixth sessions. When the war of the Rebellion broke out he "wore the grey," and was one of the fighting Southerners and not simply a politician. At the close of the war he resided in Alabama, and was appointed in 1885 by President Cleveland as United States Minister to Venezuela. He is a most affable and courteous gentleman, of fine appearance, and about fifty-eight years of age. His kind attentions to American visitors to Caracas are acknowledged most heartily by all, and are referred to with enthusiasm by those who have had the pleasure of accepting the hospitality of his house.

We were glad to learn that he is very popular here in Caracas, and is held in high esteem by President Guzman Blanco and his cabinet. Our land loses none of its brilliancy in the galaxy of nations when represented by such men as Major Scott, who, as I have already said, was one of the *fighting* and not *intriguing* rebels, and was one of the first to accept the situation manfully when defeat came, and now refers to it as "a blessing in disguise" to our great nation, binding all sections together more strongly than could have been possible before the black wall of slavery was broken down, and opening up vistas of material prosperity to the South that under the old *régime* could never have been dreamed of.

> "Sweet are the uses of adversity,
> Which, like the toad, ugly and venomous,
> Wears yet a precious jewel in his head."

Under the guidance of Major Scott we visited all the points of interest in this truly beautiful city in the mountains of Venezuela. The numerous *plazas*, or parks, are well shaded with a variety of tropical trees (none so beautiful, however, as our own lovely maples) and ornamented with fine statuary. In one of the parks is a superb bronze statue of Guzman Blanco, with an inscription which I copied and which reads as follows:

> La Paz i la libertad el order Administrativo i el Progresso
> Intellectual i material, Debidos,
> Al GENERAL GUZMAN BLANCO.
> Tanto Como La Dignidad de la Patria ante el Estranjero
> que el ha revivindicado son el Verridadero
> Pedestal De esta Estatua.

In another park called the Plaza of Santa Teresa, is a bronze statue of our Washington, erected in the centennial year of Bolivar in 1883. The inscription on it says:

> GUZMAN BLANCO,
> *Illustrious American*,
> President United States of Venezuela,
> Erected this Statue.

Another very fine statue is an equestrian one in bronze of General Simon Bolivar, the great "Liberator" of these South American States. The Venezuelans celebrate the anniversary of his birth, the same as we do the twenty-second day of February, the birthday of our own Washington.

A public garden called Calvario is on a hill a half mile or so from the city. It is the gift of President Guzman Blanco to the City of Caracas, and a place of wonderful beauty.

BRONZE STATUE OF GENERAL BOLIVAR.

Caracas, though up in the mountains three thousand five hundred feet above the level of the Caribbean Sea, is yet in a lovely valley nine miles long by two miles wide, while towering above it on every side are the majestic mountains sending down their cool streams of water for the uses of the city. From this garden of Calvario a magnificent view of the city, the valley, and the panorama of mountains is obtained. Major Scott took us also through all the cathedrals, the public buildings, the gallery of paintings, and also to the Pantheon where are buried all the dead heroes of Venezuelan history.

Mentioning to the president our presence in the city, General Guzman Blanco at once signified to Major Scott his desire to meet us, and appointed an hour for us to visit him at his palace. Presenting ourselves at the proper time, we were escorted through a line of colored soldiers on guard to a magnificent apartment in the palace. While waiting for the president to come in, I was informed by Major Scott that I had been selected by the party (four other Americans) to be the spokesman to address the illustrious president. I protested, and pleaded my ignorance of any language but English (and but a meagre knowledge of that), but the president's secretary assured me, in well-expressed English, that he would interpret faithfully to General Blanco any remarks that I would be pleased to make.

Forsaken by my friends, who showed no signs of relenting from their cruel sentence, and fearing that I would be shot by the guards if I attempted to run away, I submitted to my fate. Just as I had braced up a little and had framed a few well-rounded sentences to throw at the president, I caught sight of myself in one of the long mirrors which adorned the room. A tropical sun on board ship had played the deuce with my face, and Bardolph's nose, at the Boar's Head Tavern, when Falstaff called him the "knight of the burning lamp," was not more fiery red than my whole countenance. I was about to make another masterly attempt at retreat, when the president was announced, and we were introduced individually by Major Scott.

Guzman Blanco is sixty years of age, is about six feet and two inches tall, has been a very handsome man and still retains much of his good looks, although his hair and moustache are gray and lines of either age or anxiety are on his face and brow. Shaking our hands cordially he expressed his pleasure at meeting citizens of that country that he so greatly admired and whose beneficent forms of government he had tried to emulate. His knowledge of English is so slight that after a few words he relapsed into Spanish, which his secretary interpreted very gracefully to us.

I then swallowed a huge lump that had grown and glued itself to my throat, and asked the secretary to please say to General Blanco that through the kind offices of Major Scott, we had been shown the many public improvements in the City of Caracas, which had been made during the years that he had been at the head of the government; that while all these had impressed us with the prosperity of his administration, we had been more profoundly impressed with the statements made to us by Major Scott and others, of the deep interest that the president had taken in the intellectual advancement of his people—that through his exertions over fifteen hundred free schools had been established in Venezuela where none had before existed—that monasteries and convents were turned into colleges, and an era of education for the masses had been successfully inaugurated, through which future generations would rise up and call him blessed. I was going on to say some more of the same sort, when a thought of my red nose and parboiled cheeks checked further utterance in that line of thought, and I concluded my remarks with an expression of the pleasure we experienced in being honored by this reception. I thought the secretary elaborated my remarks somewhat in his interpretation to the president, for the illustrious American advanced and pressed my hand as he thanked me for my "kind words." At this juncture some light refreshments and wine and cigars were served, after which we took our leave of the President of the United States of Venezuela.

That Guzman Blanco is a remarkable man goes without saying, but he has exhibited a combination of qualities rarely found in public men. He is not only a soldier, and a wonderfully good one, but he is also a statesman, and a remarkably able one. Added to these, he has been a shrewd business man and by "thrift" has accumulated a princely fortune of fifteen millions of dollars. His friends say that he is honest, wise, and a benefactor of his race. His enemies say otherwise, but the *prima facie* evidence is, that his several administrations have been characterized by great material improvements and intellectual advancement to his country and to his people. I prefer to accept this view of his character, as our friend Hamlet remarks, " Be thou as chaste as ice, as pure as snow, thou shalt not escape calumny."

THE PANTHEON, WHERE ARE BURIED THE ILLUSTRIOUS DEAD. CITY OF CARACAS, VENEZUELA.

CHAPTER XII.

MAÑANA.

> To-morrow, and to-morrow, and to-morrow,
> Creeps in this petty pace from day to day
> To the last syllable of recorded time,
> And all our yesterdays have lighted fools
> The way to dusty death.—*Macbeth*.

ONE of the words most in use in Venezuela, and indeed among all the Spanish-speaking people of tropical countries, is "*Mañana*"—pronounced in their smooth and musical language, *Mah-nyah-nah*. It means "to-morrow," and as their habit of life is one of indolence, diametrically the opposite of that of our Northern people—which is one of thrift and industry—so their proverb is practically the reverse of ours, and instead of being "never put off till to-morrow what can be done to-day," is to the effect, "never do to-day what can be done to-morrow." The enervating climate is probably the first cause of this, and successive generations go on through life as their ancestors have before them. When asked to do anything that involves physical exertion, they ejaculate "Mañana," and sit still!

"To-morrow" is their accepted time and the day of their salvation from the ills of poverty; but that "to-morrow" never comes, so they remain poor and wretched, hugging to their bosoms that delusive "to-morrow" and wasting away the "to-day" which is the only time that mortal man can call his own. They can thus be truthfully called "the people of to-morrow," for this characteristic is observable in all classes of society, though doubtless it is more pronounced among the poor and ignorant. When the masses have become more intelligent, as the free schools begin to disperse the dense clouds of ignorance and superstition, Industry will be more honored and courted, while Indolence will droop her head in shame, and then will the " Mañana " be no longer the fatal rock on which their lives are wrecked.

And so I say again, all honor to the man who, though " native here and to the manner born," has risen superior to the bias of climate and national character, and founded hundreds of free schools and scores of universities and colleges for the education of his people. The name of Guzman Blanco will always hold a prominent place in South American history as a soldier and a statesman, but it will shine the brightest as he is viewed in the light of the *educator* and consequently the greatest *benefactor* of his people.

Gloomy looking as prison walls are the exteriors of all the dwellings of Caracas, but after passing through the dismal portals, a few steps usher you into a delightful *patio* or courtyard, in which are growing in tropical luxuriance, trees and flowers, fruits and ferns, and in many instances a fountain of pure water mingles its soft murmurs with the songs of birds—making a miniature garden of Eden. Around this charming bower are the spacious apartments with their high ceilings, large windows, innocent of glass, but with heavy inside shutters to keep out the strong light and heat of mid-day. The chairs and lounges are of cane and the floors are usually bare or covered with matting. Upholstered furniture and carpets are but little used in Venezuela, though we found both, and of the richest description, in the palace of the president.

A ride one Sunday afternoon, toward evening, discovered to us many very pretty female faces at the windows. Some of my more giddy companions were inclined to flirt with the fair and jewelled señoritas, who seemed not averse to exchanging smiles with the foreigners, which filled the young New Yorkers full of conceit. But I, remembering my Bardolph complexion, could not lay the flattering unction to my soul, and cynically reflecting that "beauty is purchased by the weight," and that "ornament is but the guiled shore to a most dangerous sea," with eyes severe I kept my heart in my pocket, and returned to my hotel unharmed by Cupid's darts.

A letter of introduction to the firm of Boulton & Co., in Caracas, procured for me many polite attentions. In company with young Mr. Boulton of New York, who had been spending several months in Venezuela, I visited the coffee plantation of his uncle a few miles out of the city. The *modus operandi* of preparing the coffee for shipment was carefully explained to me. In brief it is about as follows: The coffee, when first picked in the pod, is put into a large stone vat to clean it; then thrown into the hopper of the hulling machine; the hulls drop in one place and the berry in another, which is a vat full of running water; here it is washed by stirring by the negroes to rid it of the glutinous matter attached to it. It is then shoveled out on the broad *patio* or yard, with floor of brick, to dry. Then it is shoveled into the "trillo" or "rollo," where the little skin or parchment which still adheres to it is taken off by a great wheel. Now it still has a certain amount of dust and skin clinging to it, so it must be put into a "blower," which not only thoroughly cleanses but also assorts it as to size. Then there is another machine—a Yankee invention—which takes the berries from the blower and sorts out the *flat* beans from the *round* ones. The round beans are really no better than the flat ones, but command a higher price, which seemed to me a "little trick of the trade." After all this the coffee is picked over by hand, by women, to take out every defective bean. There were twenty or thirty negro women engaged in this occupation, and some of them looked as if they had been at it ever since Columbus discovered the country.

On our return from San Bernardino, the name of Mr. Boulton's estate, we drove along the banks of a mountain stream in which were scores of women washing clothes. They beat them on the stones in a manner that must be highly destructive to buttons, if not to the texture of the garments. With their skirts tucked up in a most thorough and extensive manner, these stalwart washerwomen, as they bent down to their labor, looked like a *corps de ballet hors de combat*. Such a display of female limbs would doubtless have shocked many people who witness the gyrations of a ballet troupe with perfect equanimity, and without a thought of anything immodest or improper in the performance. "Art" is one thing, "nature" is another!

In the Casa Municipal, or City Hall, is a painting, the subject of which is the signing of the Declaration of Independence, fifth Julio, 1811. Its size is twenty-two feet by twenty feet, and it is said to be a finer work of art than the one having a similar subject, so familiar to Americans, in the rotunda of the Capitol at Washington. It was painted by a French artist, M. Tovar y Tovar, at Paris in 1883.

There are four daily papers published at Caracas. Being all printed in Spanish I derived but little comfort from them. I did, however, glean from one of them the sad news of the death of Henry Ward Beecher, which reached Caracas by the way of England and the Island of Trinidad! It was read by me about two weeks after the death occurred.

There are two clubs in Caracas, one of which, "Club Union," I visited and spent an enjoyable evening. I was introduced to a number of gentlemen there who, though native Venezuelans, addressed me in good English. I also met while in

Caracas, Señor Olavarria, a distinguished citizen greatly respected by all, and who has recently been appointed by General Blanco as Minister to the United States. He impressed me as being a man of great ability, and as his particular mission to this country is to enlist the United States in a friendly effort to settle the serious disputes between Venezuela and England, I believe that he will present the subject to our government in a way that will lead it to take some action in the premises.

There are but one hundred and fourteen miles of finished railways in all Venezuela, though there are in process of building perhaps one hundred and fifty miles more. It is a most interesting country to visit, and not a bad country to live in. Its known, but as yet undeveloped, resources are apparently boundless. There are no richer mines on the globe than in Venezuela. Its agricultural and other products give freights to many great ships, but few of which, alas, fly the American flag.

The Messrs. Boulton with their fine steamers, the "Philadelphia," the "Valencia" and the "Caracas," comprising the Red D Line, are doing a large business with this wonderfully productive country; but aside from these, I did not see or hear of another American vessel doing business at any of the ports of Venezuela. On the other hand, English, French and Spanish steamers and ships, are to be found in every port on the coast.

DEGENERATE REMAINS OF THE ONCE POWERFUL TRIBE OF CARIB INDIANS.—VENEZUELA.

CHAPTER XIII.

Homeward Bound.

THE days and evenings were so agreeably spent in Caracas that it was with extreme regret that, at the end of a week, we were obliged to say adieu to the many kind people whose acquaintance we had made, and return to La Guayra to commence our homeward voyage.

The climate of Caracas we had found delightful and lead us to applaud the wisdom of the old Spaniards, which induced them to build their beautiful cities on such heavenly heights. The people we had found both polite and generously hospitable, and we flattered ourselves that the more cultivated classes have a little warmer feeling toward the citizens of the United States, than toward any other foreign visitors to their city. Certain it is we heard nothing but words of praise and friendship for our country, its citizens and its government. Germans are also much liked in Venezuela, but the same cannot be said — so far as our observation went — of the English. There is a deep feeling of resentment toward them for the encroachment of their government upon valuable territory claimed by Venezuela, and the breach will widen rapidly unless a reasonable compromise is soon effected.

Soon after reaching La Guayra we again embarked on the steamer "Philadelphia," and the homeward voyage began. Our cargo consisted of twenty-five thousand bags of coffee, weighing one hundred and thirty pounds each, several thousand hides, large numbers of goat and deer skins, several hundred sacks of bones and divi-divi, besides bananas, salt fish, cocoa, etc. Our ship with its heavy cargo rides very steadily and all the passengers are in the best of spirits. Our invalids have become well and active, and we resume our amusements with renewed zest and thorough enjoyment.

My intimacy with Mr. Morrison resulted in his imparting to me the fact that he was a minstrel by profession, and was the part proprietor of a well-known and fashionable minstrel troupe located in New York. He assumed the name of Morrison while on this voyage to avoid any unpleasant publicity, and his *incognito* was respected by me to the end of our voyage.

And now, after six or seven days of delightful weather and smooth seas, we approach that fair land where the changing seasons are more beautiful than continual bloom and summer; where the maples are more lovely than the towering palms; where the women have the roses of health on their cheeks and the light of love and intelligence in their eyes, far excelling in their beauty all the dark-eyed señoritas of these Southern climes; where Peace reigns under a beneficent government *of* the people and *for* the people—or if grim-visaged War ever darkens that fair land, it is to preserve those grand institutions, founded on liberty and justice, which our forefathers established and bequeathed to us, and which are the ADMIRATION OF THE WORLD.

It is as we approach our dear native land from a foreign shore, that our hearts burn with love for our matchless government. As we revolve in our mind all the blessings we enjoy so largely in excess of those of any other people, we cannot help singing from the heart:

> "My native country, thee,
> Land of the noble, free,
> Thy name I love;
> I love thy rocks and rills,
> Thy woods and templed hills;
> My heart with rapture thrills
> Like that above."

The old saying, "when March comes in like a lamb it will go out like a lion," was never better verified than it was on this voyage in March, 1887. The first day of the month in New York was bright and sunshiny with moderating weather, and on the second day, when we sailed for South America, the air was soft and balmy as in June. Even outside of Sandy Hook, with a fresh breeze, no overcoat was needed, and not till the twenty-eighth of the same month, on our homeward voyage, did I again don that garment so necessary in a Northern climate at this season of the year.

On the twenty-eighth instant we caught the sun and took an observation, which showed us to be one hundred and seventy-three miles from New York. In less than an hour afterward a dense fog closed in about us, though the wind was strong from the southeast and a heavy sea was running. The fog-whistle was blown every three minutes as we steamed cautiously along. After two or three hours the fog lifted, and very suddenly the wind veered around to the westward and blew a gale. It also rained in torrents, which seemed to have the effect to beat down the waves somewhat.

The rain continued till about eight o'clock P. M., when the wind shifted to the northeast, and a blinding snow-storm set in. It also grew very cold, and soon our rigging was coated with ice and our decks covered with both snow and ice. The wind howled and shrieked through the rigging like so many demons

A SMALL SHIP IN A BIG STORM.

from the infernal regions. It was impossible to stand on the deck. If going forward toward the bow of the ship, you had to pull yourself along by anything that you could lay hold of, and if going aft, you had to hold back by the same agencies or be blown along the slippery decks in the most summary manner. A journey from the Social Hall to the wheel-house, meant hard work and a thorough drenching. I made it once, and was thereafter content to remain in the cabin or the Social Hall the rest of the night, although I did not go to sleep, but sat up to watch the progress of events.

The weather continued like this till daylight, and all through that terrible night Captain Hess stood on the bridge, guiding, so far as lay in human power, the destiny of his ship. I know some of the anxieties that weigh upon a commander's mind during such a night as this, and as I saw Captain Hess come down from the bridge, shortly after daylight, with his hair and beard and eyebrows encased with ice, I knew that he felt relieved of a load of anxiety. Darkness must greatly increase the perils of storm on the sea, for the danger of collision increases in snow-storm or fog, when no light can be seen a ship's length ahead. More especially is the danger of collision increased as any large port like that of New York is approached. But we were mercifully preserved from such disaster, and shortly after breakfast, when about forty miles from New York, we took on the pilot who had been waiting for us in his trim little schooner all through that stormy night.

We reached our dock at about two o'clock P. M., and thus ended a voyage to the Spanish Main replete with rational, and I might even say rapturous, enjoyment from first to last. My reflections in looking back upon it after a lapse of several months, lead me to wonder how people can resist the temptation to take these tropical voyages in the winter season. The transition from the keen icy blasts of the North to the warm and delicious air of the tropics, is so entrancing that even the memory of it long after is a delightful pleasure.

I have spoken of the excellent accommodations of the steamer "Philadelphia," and the uniform courtesy of her officers, and I have been informed by frequent travelers by this line, that the steamers "Valencia" and "Caracas" of the same line are nearly, if not quite, equal in all their appointments and equally well officered. I am quite ready to believe this, for the gentlemen who are at the head of this long-established line of steamers, are men of great experience, knowing full well how to meet all the requirements of travelers by ocean, and sparing no pains or expense to make their steamers thoroughly comfortable, and as safe as human agency can devise.

CHAPTER XIV.

The Story of Toussaint L'Ouverture.

IN a retrospective glance at the history of the West India Islands and the other former possessions of Spain in North, Central, and South America, from their discovery in the latter part of the fifteenth century to the present time—when only the islands of Cuba, Porto Rico and Isle of Pines remain in her grasp—we see a long list of illustrious names, comprising eminent navigators, soldiers and statesmen.

The central figure in this group of historic characters, is, of course, "Cristobal Colon," or, as he is known in American history, Christopher Columbus. His story is familiar to all as a household word, and need not be referred to here, but there are other great men who figured prominently in the history of these Spanish-American countries, whose exploits are not so familiar, and I have ventured to select two of them to be the subjects of short biographical sketches, which shall conclude this volume.

The Story of Toussaint L'Ouverture.

Hayti, the native name of this gem of the Antilles, signifies, in the Caribbean tongue, a land of *high hills*. Columbus called it, in admiration of its beauty, Hispaniola, or Little Spain. The French and English gave currency to its principal historical title St. Domingo, from its chief city.

The Caribbean race, humanely treated by the great navigator, afterwards speedily vanished under the merciless rigors of the gold mines. Then, in the greedy strife of France and Spain, the dark and melancholy era of African slavery opened upon those luxuriant shores.

Next to Cuba, Hayti is one of the richest and most beautiful of the Greater Antilles, abounding in mineral resources of large variety, and favored with pleasing and serviceable diversities of climate. Its western portion, ceded by Spain to France in 1797, rose to so high a state of agricultural fertility as to have supplied Europe with half its consumed sugar.

Amidst the luxuriance of these tropical scenes, the justly celebrated hero and patriot, Toussaint L'Ouverture, was born in 1743. Early in childhood so marked was his physical delicacy, that even the hope of his raising was despaired of. But, subsequently, he strengthened and hardened into a youth of exceptional vigor, agility and endurance. He could run, it is said, like an antelope ; and when mounted on the wildest and fleetest horse, he was a miniature Alexander.

He is credibly stated to have been the grandson of a powerful and virtuous African monarch ; who, perhaps, transmitted to him not a few of the noble traits of character that his mature life displayed. As a slave, it was his great privilege to fall into the hands of an overseer, M. Bayon, of uncommon kindness; who, among other things, encouraged him to learn to read and write, acquirements that largely contributed to his ultimate power, as his tongue and pen proved no less serviceable to him than his sword. And most munificently did he repay the benefit. For when the great insurrection, 1791, burst upon the island, M. Bayon being on the point of falling into the hands of the infuriated negroes, the faithful Toussaint securely embarked him and his family on board a ship for America ; furnished, also, with many hogsheads of sugar for their immediate and prospective necessities.

On a neighboring plantation there lived a virtuous black, Pierre Baptiste by name, who stood godfather to the little Toussaint at his baptism; and who afterwards sedulously instructed him in religion, as well as taught him, to some extent, both French and Latin. And under such wise and humane culture, the young African grew up to manhood; and when duly married and installed in his humble cabin, what could furnish a more pleasing image of his virtuous and contented life, than the description of it incidentally given by himself to a casual traveler?

"We went," said he, "to labor in the fields, my wife and I, hand in hand. Scarcely were we conscious of the fatigues of the day. Heaven always blessed our toil. Not only had we abundance for ourselves, but we had the pleasure of giving food to blacks who needed it. On the Sabbath, and on festival days, we went to church, my wife, my parents, and myself. Returning to our cottage, after a pleasant meal, we passed the remainder of the day as a family, and we closed it by prayer, in which all took part."

The immediate occasion of the great Insurrection of St. Domingo, was an appeal made to the slaves by the free mulattoes, who deemed themselves politically misused by the whites. This appeal fell like a burning coal in a magazine of powder, awaking the slaves, *en masse*, from their long torpor. And upon the night air of August 21, 1791, terrific indeed was the tocsin that sounded out, "*Kill, burn and destroy*," being the watchword that flew, with lightning speed, over the hills and through the valleys of the beautiful land. But in a drama so sanguinary, Toussaint would have neither hand nor voice. His soul revolted at acts so extreme; and he bravely stood personal guard over the shivering family of his benignant overseer. At the same time he was fully prepared to co-operate with his race, so soon as the project of their freedom could be reduced to humane and warrantable limits.

Having been a diligent reader of the works of the famous Abbé Raynal, Toussaint had imbibed from them fixed and intelligent principles on the great topic of human liberty. And particularly had he noticed the prediction of that eminent writer, that a vindicator of negro wrongs would ultimately arise out of the bosom of the negro race. But the ripeness of over fifty years was upon him, before he dared seriously to think of himself as possibly that vindicator. Leaders of no small worth and valor had preceded him—Biasson, Bouknant, Jean Francois, and the like. But in the admiration, confidence and trust of his dusky fellow-strugglers, he speedily outdistanced them all. He is described as possessed of a fine eye, rapid and penetrating in its glances; sober by rigid habit; incessant and untiring in activity, and astute and judicious in all his plans and movements. In the military tactics of the island, neither Spain, France, nor England, ever long succeeded in outgeneraling him. And this credit is fully accorded him by French chroniclers, who, otherwise, were glad to detract from his merits. They speak of him as an excellent horseman, traveling with surprising rapidity from point to point. To the ignorant negroes he seemed as if superior to time and space. He and his swift-galloping horse appeared in their eyes as almost one compound being. As a general, he was the unrivalled idol of his troops, and even by observers of an higher social grade, he was not unfrequently likened to some great and noted captain of other lands and times.

Long wearied by the clashing arms of Spain and France for the possession of his native island, he at length cast his lot unreservedly with France; only, however, with the distinct understanding and proviso, that the enslavement of his people was to be forever a thing of the past. On this point he was inflexible. He carried on his heart the pregnant sentence of Abbé Raynal, "*Liberty is everyone's own property.*" And from this he never swerved, though a most faithful servant of France, through all the changing phases of her government.

The French commissioners he uniformly received with all due respect; but, at the same time, checkmated all their plots to re-establish the African servitude.

The extraordinary abilities of this remarkable man, crossing the Atlantic, caused the French powers, in 1797, to commission him general-in-chief of all the armies of St. Domingo. And this was subsequently confirmed by Napoleon, and continued until Leclerc, the pampered husband of Pauline, Napoleon's sister, appeared on the scene. This man was sent out, if possible, to seduce this colonial patriot; or, at all events, by some means, to capture him; a mistake that eventually cost France the loss of the beautiful island, and gave there to Leclerc himself an inglorious grave.

No one could allege that Toussaint's administration of the affairs of the island had not been most felicitous. Refugee planters to the United States came back, by his invitation, to their former homes, and were faithfully protected. Upon all employers of the negroes, he enjoined moderation in discipline, and liberality in food and sustenance. He sought, also, all reasonable means of reconciling these laborers to their lot, encouraging them to application and industry. He made laws against idleness and vagrancy, and enforced them with rigor. He fostered, also, education and religion. And so the long blood-stained and war-scarred island rapidly put on a smiling and happy face.

At this juncture England, at war with France, dispatched thither assaulting fleets and armies. But these hostile attempts were all admirably met by the skillful and every-where-present Toussaint. His allegiance to France never faltered. This was so conspicuous that even the ill-natured Dubroca was constrained to testify of him, that "his conduct during the war with the English was brilliant, and without a stain." The first consul himself also wrote him, that "if the colors of the French people fly on St. Domingo, it is to you and your brave blacks that we owe it."

But, in the midst of all this, Napoleon, loosed from his European wars by the peace of Amiens, suddenly dispatched an army of 20,000 men to re-establish in Hayti the hated human slavery. He sought to conceal his design. But all his duplicity, and that of his emissaries, failed to blind the eyes of Toussaint. He distinctly announced to them all that, while remaining loyal to France, he should also be true to the freedom of his race, and that on this line the remaining battle of his life would be fought out. And there he stood, like a stag at bay, until the basest of treachery stole him from his family and his people, and shut him up in a foreign fortress to die. But, by a just Nemesis, the perfidious Leclerc must die too, for the "Yellow Jack" ere long clutched him, and interred his fetid bones in the soil of the land that he had so shamefully sought to enslave.

Napoleon, it is said, could never forgive the innocently spoken words of Toussaint, duly reported to him, that "if Bonaparte is the first man in France, Toussaint is the first man in the Archipelago of the Antilles." Such an one the haughty Corsican could no longer endure. By some means, fair or foul, his downfall must be accomplished. From a project so unworthy, the French Minister Vincent has the solitary distinction of trying to dissuade his master, receiving only, in answer, the sentence of banishment to the island of Elba; the identical spot, singularly enough, to which the lofty tyrant was himself subsequently banished.

An artful letter addressed to Toussaint as "Citizen General," in which Napoleon flatters him in high strains, concludes with this remarkable tribute: "And you, General, are the first of your color that has reached such an height of power, and that has gained such distinction by bravery and military talent."

But the sole aim of all this chicanery was to remove Toussaint out of the path of his nefarious designs upon the liberty of the blacks. With this powerful chief on the island, the first consul saw no possible restoration of slavery. Hence the necessity of his removal. And the accomplishment of this base project was the *chef-d'œuvre* of the knavish Leclerc. Decoyed, in the most deceitful manner, from the quiet and security of his home, on the pretext of a friendly interview, Toussaint suddenly found himself surrounded by a troop of armed men, and himself solitary. With the instinct of a soldier, he drew his sword; but, upon a moment's reflection, he sheathed it again, with these tranquil, and also prophetic, words: "The justice of Heaven will avenge my cause"— amply afterwards fulfilled, if not elsewhere, at least on the rocky islet of St. Helena.

Then quickly followed his transfer to a French frigate, his transit across the Atlantic, his imprisonment at Paris, and his final incarceration within the gloomy walls of the Joux, amid the deep recesses of the Jura Mountains.

Against such perfidy and cruelty the poor captive pleaded in vain. The dampness of his dungeon, and his systematic starvation, rapidly wasted him away. All his most touching appeals to Paris were in vain. He might as well have spoken to the mute walls or mountains around him. His destiny was sealed. The supplies of food became more and more scanty; all his wants were neglected, until at last, the fountain of his life utterly exhausted, the inhuman jailer found him, early in April, 1803, silent in death.

The news of his death, in Hayti, was soon followed by desperate uprisings of the people, and by the expulsion of the

French. Also, intestine wars spread over the land. The fierce strife of races, colors, and different sections of the island, under great leaders like Dessalines, Christophe, Petiore, Boyer and others, is painful to reflect upon; although it consoles us to think that, under the merciful guidance of a Supreme Power, they ultimately resulted in the final and permanent deliverance of Hayti from the thraldom of African slavery.

Our hero, Toussaint, known in early life by his baptismal name of François Dominique, has passed into history as Toussaint L'Ouverture. Of the origin of this latter title, accounts somewhat vary. The most common of these is, that General Lareaux, noticing the facility with which Toussaint brushed aside difficulties in his path, said to certain around him, "*Cet homme fait ouverture partout,*" meaning that he was capable of making an *opening*, or way, for himself and his cause under all circumstances. And from this incident "L'Ouverture," or the *opening*, became permanently attached to his name. The talented Lamartine inclined to "L'Aurora," the *day-break*, said to have been suggested by a monk, who thus distinguished Toussaint as the *morning star* of Haytien freedom. Still a third account is that given by Lacroix, that Toussaint himself, independently, assumed the title, to signify thereby to his race and people that he felt assured that he could *open* to them the door of a better future, if they would follow him. And to this last we confess ourselves inclined to give in our adherence.

As to the general character of this great man, no estimate of it could be just that failed to place it high. In his determined revolt against the servitude of his race, he had all the fire and energy of Spartacus, with vastly more of self-restraint and humanity. As a patriot and liberator, he was one of whom Bolivar, himself, need not have been ashamed, while he had not a tithe of Bolivar's social advantages to lift him to his eminence. In the untaught skill with which he foiled the trained hosts of Spain, France and England, he reminds us of Wallace and Bruce, or even of Alfred the Great. And we should not shame even the Roman Cincinnatus by naming them in company. Those who knew him best, scarcely set any bounds to their admiration of his works and worth.

His pledged word of fidelity was so well recognized, that it was never questioned or distrusted. Of this a noticeable instance occurred in the case of the British General Maitland, who ventured to visit Toussaint at his camp in the mountains during the English war with France. The French commissioner, Roume, snatching at so rare an opportunity, wrote a hasty letter to Toussaint to capture General Maitland. Soon after Maitland reached the camp Toussaint came in, and handed him two letters, saying, "There, General, read these, before we talk together. The one is a letter just received from Roume and the other my answer. I would not come to you till I had written my answer to him, that you may see how safe you are with me and how incapable I am of baseness." Like Juba, the Numidian prince in Addison's "Cato," he could say:

> "Better to die a thousand deaths,
> Than wound my honor."

Above all, he was devoutly and most honestly religious: as the Spanish Marquis D'Hermona, who knew him intimately, said of him, somewhat extravagantly perhaps, "If the Heavenly Being were to descend upon earth, he could not inhabit a heart more apparently good than that of Toussaint."

On the whole, then, observing this remarkable man from first to last, or surveying him from head to foot, as Brutus said of Cæsar, that he was "the foremost man of all this world," so we may not hesitate to pronounce TOUSSAINT L'OUVERTURE, THE "FOREMOST MAN" OF ALL THE NEGRO RACE KNOWN TO HISTORY.

CHAPTER XV.

Don Francisco Pizarro, Discoverer and Conqueror of Peru, and its First Viceroy.

THE life and adventures, discoveries and exploits, of this celebrated Spanish explorer and military commander, during the era of South America's invasion and subjection to European rule, are of remarkable historic and even romantic interest. There are scenes disclosed in his record, as given by old writers, and by our own Prescott, in his exhaustive and admirable "History of the Conquest of Peru," so novel to other ages and regions, that they strike on the mind almost as fairy tales of the "Arabian Nights." As we read chapters describing the civilization, arts, public works, and, specially, the *gold* of the ancient Peruvians, which no other nation in the world ever had in such abundance, we do not marvel that that part of the New World should have excited the cupidity of its Castilian invaders to the utmost, and induced them to make such terrible sacrifices to seize on this tempting *El Dorado*, while we deplore the fate, at their rapacious hands, of so noble a race and so fair and beautiful a kingdom.

Our limits will not, however, permit much detail of facts in the present sketch, and, referring our readers who desire more particulars to Mr. Prescott's full pages, and to the unique, learned and brilliant volume, by Ignatius Donelly, called "Atlantis," that vast sunken island of antiquity, described by Plato, we must content ourselves with presenting a brief *résumé* of Pizarro's career, and his Peruvian discoveries and acquisitions.

Francisco Pizarro, the oldest of several brothers who followed him to South America and also became famous there, was born in the City of Truxillo in the Province of Estremadura, Spain, whence he came to Panama, as early as Cortez, but did not rise to reputation as quickly. His first expedition sailed from that port in November, 1524, associated with Diego de Almagro, another great explorer and soldier. They had but one ship and one hundred and nineteen men, and this attempt to enter the land of the Incas was entirely unsuccessful. Nor more so at first, was his second expedition, which was reinforced by another hundred of his countrymen and some Indians.

Having arrived at a marshy, watery place, where the people lived in trees, they repulsed the invaders, called them the scum of the seas, and would admit none in their country who wore beards. The inhabitants made a great show of precious stones and gold. Pizarro's men now became discouraged, but he did not lose hope, and would not suffer any to return or even to write to Panama, although word got to the governor there of this state of things, when he decreed that no man should stay with Pizarro against his will. Subsequently, for awhile, he was reduced to great straits for food, etc., with his remaining followers. But fortune soon smiled upon him, and he succeeded in obtaining a foothold in a rich country, with a dignified king, named Atahualpa. This empire, called Quichua by its citizens, Pizarro named Peru, and soon after returned to Spain, whither he had before transmitted a "relation" of his important discoveries, and on this visit the Emperor Charles V. gave him the proud title of Adelantado of Peru.

Going back now with his three brothers, Fernando, Juan and Garsalo, he again was joined at Panama by Almagro—although offended that Pizarro had taken all the honor of discoveries to himself when in Spain—and set out on an expedition against the unfortunate Atahalipa, as his name is sometimes spelled, defeated his army and took him prisoner, capturing also the island of Puma. The captured king, however, ransomed himself by an amount of gold that filled a high and spacious room. The spoil was then divided among Pizarro's men, and never any soldiers in the world were richer than his. He also dealt justly with Almagro and gave him what was his due share. But, although gold was so plenty, what they needed to buy was, of course, dearer, viz.: a shirt cost £10, a quart of wine £5 and a house £250. Many soldiers returned, some with 30,000 and some with 40,000 ducats in plate. But alas for poor Atahalipa! After having thus stripped him and his subjects, and, finally, accused of treachery on evidence by no means decisive, he was led to execution, and "thus by the death of a vile malefactor, perished the last of the Incas!" Before his death, having been instructed by the missionaries of the Catholic Church, as to the nature of the sacred rite, he desired to be baptized, and was christened Juan de Atahualpa, on account of its being St. John the Baptist's day when it took place.

It was not without the pretext of extending the faith and spiritual blessings of Christendom, that the Spaniards prosecuted their conquests, and, in answer to the Peruvian chief, "why they had come to those shores?" Pizarro replied, "that he was the vassal of the greatest king of the world, and had come to assert his master's lawful supremacy, as, also, to rescue the Peruvians from the worship of the evil spirit, and to give them the knowledge of the true and only God, and of Jesus Christ, in whom to believe was salvation." "In the name of the Prince of Peace," says the eloquent Dr. Robertson, in his "History of the New World," "they ratified a contract of which plunder and bloodshed were the object." The massacre of thousands of his unarmed and unresisting subjects around him, when their king was seized for the last time, forms one of the darkest chapters in the annals of time. The innocent Peruvians, before the sad lessons of experience taught them better, had imagined that, as they had never done any harm to the Spaniards, none would be done to them.

As an all-important objective point, Pizarro soon took possession of Cuzco, the chief city of Peru, where he found immense wealth. So plenty was gold, that it was reported that even the kitchen utensils in most houses were of that precious metal, and the tiles of their roofs. One of their palaces had an artificial garden, the soil of which was made of small pieces of fine gold, which was artificially planted with different kinds of maize, having golden stems, leaves and ears, and placed in it twenty sheep, with lambs and shepherds, four llamas, ten women of full size, all of gold, and a cistern of gold that excited universal wonder. This agrees with Plato's picture of ancient mythical Atlantis. The most renowned temple was at Cuzco, the interior of which was literally a mine of gold. On the walls was emblazoned a representation of the Deity, consisting of a human countenance looking forth from innumerable rays of light.

It is related that the old Peruvian name of the Supreme Being, the Creator, was *Virachocha*, or *Pachacamac*. They called jewels the "tears wept from the sun." The value of such as adorned the great temple at Cuzco, was computed at 180 millions of dollars. But the Peruvians did not value gold and silver so much as money as for sacred uses. This remarkable people had made great advances in the arts, and particularly in architecture, like the ancient Egyptians, with whom they had other points of resemblance, *e. g.*, in the worship of the sun, moon and planets, the soul's immortality, resurrection of the dead, division of the year, castes as in India, triumphal arches for returning heroes, agricultural interests, etc.

But we must now speak of the civilization and architectural remains of this wonderful race. Says Baldwin, in his "Ancient America," "This whole region, as found by the Spaniards, was a prosperous and populous empire, and presented a notable development of some of the more important arts of civilized life." Pizarro's company found everywhere traces of a civilization of vast antiquity, Cyclopean building stones, and gateways of stone thirty feet long, fifteen feet wide and six feet thick. In the ancient capital of the Chimus, in North Peru, which remains to this day, its ruins covering not less than twenty square miles, are found pyramidal structures half a mile in circumference, massive walls, each with its water tank, etc. Around Lake Titicaca are great buildings of brown stone, having doors and windows, with posts, sills and thresholds of stone, in modern New York City style. At Cuelap there is a wall 3,600 feet long, 560 feet broad, and 150 feet high, on the top of which another lofty one pierces the sky. There are, also, near Huamango, aqueducts and public roads across sierras and rivers, some over suspension bridges, and one road, from Cuzco to Chili, hundreds of miles long. Of this, Humboldt, the celebrated traveler and savant, says: "The road was marvelous; none of the Roman roads I had seen in Italy, the south of France, or in Spain, appeared to me more imposing than this work of the ancient Peruvians." These structures are said to have been built before the time of the Incas. So, also, their products in cotton and wool are said to have exceeded in fineness anything known in Europe at that time. As to these accumulations of wealth, it is related that in twenty-five years after the conquest, the Spaniards sent eight hundred millions of dollars to old Spain. Pizarro himself had the chair or throne of the Incas, which was of solid gold.

But to revert once more to the awful massacre of the unsuspecting thousands by this ferocious conqueror, when their monarch, Atahualpa, was captured to be spared but for a brief space, we would say that this booty was bought at a sacrifice of honor and good faith, such as all history can scarcely parallel. And although it is true that the last of the Incas had, in securing his own imperial station, committed fearful atrocities, this fact did not justify the perfidy of the Spaniards in seizing his person for their prey, and his public execution at their hands. But a day of Providential retribution was near, in the form of a dire civil war among the invaders themselves, in which the slain were many, and Pizarro one of them. He had quarreled with and put to death his early friend, Almagro, and resisted the authority of Peter de la Gasca, whom the emperor of Spain had sent to quell the revolts in Peru, and empowered to right the wrongs of that injured people. His death was in Quito, and one of violence, when desperately resisting those whose mission was his execution, and "Jesu!" was the last utterance of his lips. Yet his faithful biographer, the historian of the conquest, Prescott, does not give him the credit of the religious sincerity and zeal for propagating the faith, of Cortez, his kinsman, the conqueror of Mexico.

The predominant passion of Pizarro was undoubtedly the thirst for gold and dominion at any cost. Yet he was brave by nature, and endowed with courage to face unexampled difficulties. His march across the Andes was heroic. His speech to his soldiers, at that time, is worthy of commemoration, viz.: "Let every one of you take courage to go forward like a good soldier. God fights for his own. Doubt not He will humble the power of the heathen, and bring them to the knowledge of the true faith, the great object of the conquest." His birth is supposed to have been about A. D. 1471—he came to the New World several years before his invasion of Peru—and his death occurred not far from the year 1546. The people he was the instrument of conquering, were in every respect a grand and powerful race, and without their fire-arms and horses, the Spaniards never could have subdued them. Their laws were almost agrarian with respect to landed property, their institutions just, and their faith in a future world of discrimination between the good and the bad, was such as the ancient Egyptians held to, and which, probably, many who "profess and call themselves Christians" do not any more practically regard. And, says Mr. Prescott, familiar with all the old Spanish records of the Peruvians by learned and pious Roman Catholic priests, "They had attained to the sublime conception of one Great Spirit, the Creator and Ruler of the universe." The frontispiece of his noble work presents an engraved likeness of Pizarro, from an original full-length painting in the Palace of the Incas, at Lima.

On a column at Truxillo, Spain, his birth-place, are to be found the following lines, by the celebrated English poet Southey, which condensed in a small compass the more remarkable traits of Pizarro's character, and with them we conclude the present imperfect sketch:

> PIZARRO HERE WAS BORN; A GREATER NAME
> THE LIST OF GLORY BOASTS NOT. TOIL AND PAIN,
> FAMINE AND HOSTILE ELEMENTS AND HOSTS
> EMBATTLED, FAILED TO CHECK HIM IN HIS COURSE,
> NOT TO BE WEARIED, NOT TO BE DETERRED,
> NOT TO BE OVERCOME. A MIGHTY REALM
> HE OVERRAN, AND WITH RESISTLESS ARM,
> SLEW OR ENSLAVED ITS UNOFFENDING SONS,
> AND WEALTH, AND POWER, AND FAME, MADE HIS REWARDS.
> THERE IS ANOTHER WORLD BEYOND THE GRAVE,
> ACCORDING TO THEIR DEEDS, WHERE MEN ARE JUDGED.
> O, READER! IF THY DAILY BREAD BE EARNED
> BY DAILY LABOR—YEA, HOWEVER LOW—
> HOWEVER WRETCHED BE THY LOT ASSUMED,
> THANK THOU, WITH DEEPEST GRATITUDE, THE GOD
> WHO MADE THEE, THAT THOU ART NOT SUCH AS HE.

www.ingramcontent.com/pod-product-compliance
Lightning Source LLC
Chambersburg PA
CBHW020059170426
43199CB00009B/340